The Courage Factor
A Collection of Presidential Essays

The Courage Factor
A Collection of Presidential Essays

R. Kirby Godsey
President, Mercer University

MERCER
UNIVERSITY PRESS

ISBN 0-86554-986-9   MUP/H671

The Courage Factor: A Collection of Presidential Essays
©2005 Mercer University Press
1400 Coleman Avenue
Macon, Georgia 31207 USA
All rights reserved
Printed in the United States of America
First edition, December 2005

The paper used in this publication meets the minimum
requirements of American National Standard
for Information Sciences—Permanence of Paper
for Printed Library Materials, ANSI Z39.48-1992. ∞

Library of Congress Cataloging-in-Publication Data

Godsey, R. Kirby (Raleigh Kirby), 1936–   .
    The courage factor : a collection of presidential
essays / R. Kirby Godsey. — 1st ed.
    ISBN-13: 978-0-86554-986-9 (hardcover : alk. paper)
    ISBN-10: 0-86554-986-9 (hardcover : alk. paper)
    1. Universities and colleges—Social aspects.
2. Education, Higher—Social aspects. I. Title.
    LC191.2.G63   2005
    378.01—dc22
                                          2005020706

Contents

Preface

The quiet responsibility that underlies every other agenda for the president of a college or any enterprise worthy to be called a corporation is to think. Even so, the relentless call to action often eclipses the time to reflect, to ponder the issues on which we are called to make decisions.

Before becoming president of Mercer University, I served as dean of a college. When I took that post, I was told that the role of the faculty was to think and the role of the president was to make speeches, and that if I were to succeed as dean, I needed to understand that the role of the dean was to keep the faculty from making speeches and to keep the president from thinking.

Well, thinking, especially for a college president, can be a dangerous precedent to set. But think we must, for the power of thought is the most important weapon in our human arsenal if we are to overcome the barbaric march of ignorance in our world.

In a world scarred by deadly conflict and rampant intolerance, ignorance remains our most insatiable enemy. People sometimes commit atrocities because of evil, malevolent hearts. More often, however, we inflict hurt and destruction because we are afraid and we are ignorant of more thoughtful and reasonable means of resolving human conflicts.

For more than twenty-five years, I have served as the president of Mercer University, a work which I have undertaken as both a high honor and a sense of deep purpose. Twice each year, during these twenty-five years, I have prepared for Mercer's board of trustees a "Report on the State of the University." For reasons that are not entirely explicable, my custom has been to begin each report with an essay or a commentary on subjects that have ranged from war to religion and from the idea of a university to the priorities that should guide the work of a university.

I was prompted to offer these reflections for several reasons. First a learning place, especially a college or university, celebrates the power of thought. The most egregious of human ills are likely to yield only to the power and creativity of the human mind. Above all else, the University was founded as a place to hold high the canons of thought and the power of the intellect to make a difference in human affairs. It is easy to become so preoccupied with the chores of higher education that we neglect the heart of our reason for being. We exist first and foremost to celebrate the capacity of the human mind and the human spirit to change the world.

Second, I have written these essays as a means of focusing my own work and a symbolic means of reminding the governing board that the most important task of the president is to provide reflective and thoughtful leadership for this enterprise called learning. It is not enough to solve problems or even to raise money. Underlying other responsibilities for leadership is to think about issues that affect the destiny of our institutions and our fragile civilization. Human civilization remains in its infancy. While colleges and universities are not likely the saviors of civilization, they play a critical role in preserving the possibility that we can continue to advance and not become consumed by our own baser interests. I believe education can provide hope and healing in a world that is mired in despair and the maladies of ignorance.

My colleagues on the board of trustees have indulged me as I have thought and written on a wide range of subjects in the belief that our university and our society is made richer if we can cultivate our capacity for public discourse. In the traditions of public discourse, you, the reader, will find that these essays explore recurring themes and ideas. I simply beg your indulgence when repetitions occur within the text.

I do not write believing that my views are superior or remotely more meaningful than those who have the grace to read what I have to say. Indeed, the more important point is to foster conversation and debate so that, in the fires of conflicting viewpoints, we can refine the truth and find common ground on which to build our life together.

I have entitled this collection of essays "The Courage Factor." The title essay regards the *Columbia* shuttle disaster and served as a tribute to those valiant men and women who gave their lives in the advance of human civilization as they pursued the edges of human discovery. But the title is also meant to point the reader toward the character of these essays as a whole. You and I live in a time and in a world where hope itself requires courage. Whatever else defines our work, educators are peddlers of hope. We believe in the difference that educated young minds can and will make in the condition of our world.

The people we educate will be able to see farther and solve some of the knotty problems that you and I have left unsolved. While they are the children of our history, they also bear the hope and the promise of a new generation. What will be required of them is a measure of courage, the courage to engage, the courage to face into the challenges that beset us, the courage to think, the courage to collaborate, the courage to reimagine the world and ultimately the courage to make a difference. The courage factor will enable them to achieve peace, to cure disease, and to bring light into a world that continues to be haunted by dreadful shadows. Only the courage factor will keep hope alive.

- 1 -

Terrorism, Religion, and the Calling of a University

As we face the fallout and fright of terrorism, we are left somewhat undone and bewildered, unable to make sure sense of these new realities. In our report to the board of trustees, issued two years before September 11, 2001, I commented that the gravest threat to human civilization is the rise of international terrorism. Terrorism sustained by religious fervor is a powerful and deadly force. In human history, it may turn out that more wars have been fought over religious territory than geographic territory.

Rising out of the ashes of this tragic episode, September 11 has occasioned a visible and palpable renewal of the American spirit. By almost any measure, America has emerged during the last century as the leader of the world order by creating an environment that is remarkably free and open both economically and socially. Diversity and dissent are a part of the strengths of the American nation while the tolerance of dissent and the commitment to an open society have now become a part of America's vulnerability. The pettiness of some of our political debates stood out in sudden stark relief against the tragedies of September 11. For a moment, we put our ideological differences aside, and we felt like one people, mourning a tragedy that violated all of our consciences.

The United States of America probably remains the most important social and governance initiative ever undertaken. As a nation, we have designed a social order built around balancing freedom and justice, fostering among free people a common respect for law and the systems of justice. America is a resilient nation, and I believe that freedom will prevail because it springs from a deep and abiding desire within the human spirit. The yearning for freedom is indeed an eternal flame. But maintaining a free society carries with it an abundance of risks, and those of us especially who have a stake in the traditions of learning must realize that these risks are unlikely to be managed without the creative power of education. Military strength will not be enough.

If we could think of the world's population as a village of one hundred people, fifty-seven of this world's village would be Asians. Twenty-one would be Europeans. Fourteen would be North and South Americans. Seventy percent of the village would be nonwhite, and seventy percent would be non-Christians. Six of the one hundred would possess sixty percent of the world's wealth. One, only one, would have a college education. So, living in an affluent and well-educated society does, in some ways, make our nation even more vulnerable. The very presence of this advanced and wealthy society intimidates and threatens so many people in the world.

Millions of people who have lost out politically and economically turn to religious belief as a means of coping with their condition. Through twisted forms of religion, the economic outcasts find their last gasp of hope in their convictions that they are on God's side, and the people of the free and wealthy West are enemies of God.

Terrorism and religion constitute an interwoven fabric. I believe the work of the University must play a significant role in building a future of hope. Our overarching responsibility is to strengthen the power of reason and to encourage the search for religious understanding in a world where fear and hatred have become dominant forces in the human village.

Throughout human history, wars have plagued and sometimes defeated the steady march of civilization. Wars are spawned by people who become consumed by a radical fear, springing from the oppressive limits of our natural human boundaries. It turns out that religion is one of mankind's principal means of coping with the uncertainties and anxieties that emerge from bumping up against our human boundaries. Perhaps, the two most powerful of life's boundaries are the mystery of death and the impenetrable barrier of standing over against another human self or society of people.

The boundaries of land and the limits of financial power are the tangible representations of the more basic and profound boundaries that claim and limit all of our lives. People tend to get defined by the land they own and the assets they possess. Yet, land and money are mostly symbols of self-identity and the human capacity to sustain life. The loss of land or money may indeed put well-being and comfort at risk. On the other hand, the loss of meaning and self-identity puts life and our reason for being alive at risk. Above all else, religious faith grants meaning, a reason for being here. Whenever people or social orders or other faiths threaten to undercut our reason for being, holy war, not simply war, holy war results.

Holy wars are the most vicious of all wars. Because the enemies are the enemies of God, the annihilation of the enemy becomes a holy act, and the sacrificial death of the holy warrior is often celebrated as a sacred event.

Holy wars are, in all candor, a common perversion of faith, and they spring from religious devotion, which has its roots in the coalescence of fear and arrogance. A vision of God that is shaped by fear is radically different from a faith that is born of grace. This perversion of religious belief has occurred in all the world's great religions—Christianity,

Judaism, Islam, and Hinduism. Three of the world's major religions, Christianity, Judaism, and Islam, were all born in the Middle East and have profoundly common roots. They belong, in a sense, to the same family of faith. Jews and Christians and Muslims are spiritual and ethnic kin. Family feuds are the worst kind, and these feuds have gone on for so long that the antagonists have long since lost any sense of springing from common roots.

Misguided and abusive forms of faith are not a new phenomenon. The current perverted version of the Muslim notion of Jihad, the Middle Ages Christian Crusades, the Roman Catholic inquisitions, and indeed some of the terrorism recorded in the Old Testament are distorted and reprehensible forms of religious devotion. Jihad and holy wars are rarely holy. "Holy war" may be the ultimate oxymoron.

While the war which America is now waging against terrorism can be seen as a right and appropriate response to an unprecedented assault, and even a responsible pursuit of justice and accountability, we should not overstep our need for justification by calling it "holy" war. The creative process of achieving civilization is far from complete. The killings that result from human warfare bear dramatic testimony—even when justified as the best that can be done during a time of repelling violence—that human beings often become victims of an inhuman cycle of violence.

Violent religion has become a frightful scourge in our world. Unfortunately, religious violence is not limited to any one of the world's religions. Throughout history, people of faith have killed in the name of God. The violence of Christianity became most visibly expressed in the Crusades of the Middle Ages. The Christian church undertook cultural and territorial conquests under the notion that these wars were holy and that overthrowing the infidels was doing God's will.

The contemporary interpretation of Jihad on the part of fundamentalist Muslims is very much akin to the spirit and character of the Middle Ages Christian Crusades. In fact, many Muslims in the world are living culturally and economically in the Middle Ages. Some Muslims are waging war on behalf of God in the same manner and spirit as did the Christians in the Middle Ages. In each case, those who die in these holy causes are either Christian or Muslim martyrs. The weapons of the twenty-first century are far more deadly, and indeed the world is far more populated, but the instincts that drove the Christian Crusades then and the twisted version of Islamic Jihad now are virtually identical. Both offer the rationale that "If our God is right, and our God is the only holy God, I can demonstrate my loyalty to God by destroying those who follow other gods."

Moreover, the Jewish and Christian idea of a "just war" is very similar to the Islamic concept of Jihad. Unlike the current uses of the term "Jihad" by radical fundamentalists, the original Muslim notion of Jihad was a corollary to the "just war." In both cases, the criteria generally include

(1) just cause (defensive wars only);
(2) last resort (all negotiations have failed);
(3) limited objectives (total destruction unwarranted); and
(4) noncombatant immunity (civilians, children are immune).

In reality, whenever these respective believers become intoxicated with irrational religious fervor, all these criteria are rationalized away. It turns out that there is no hatred like religious hatred.

In the case of each of the major world religions that have influenced the West and the Middle East, the notion and the pursuit of holy war have been rooted in a concept of religion that is meant more to protect than a religion meant to set free.

Radical fear becomes the compelling rationale for faith. It is the fear of death, the fear of people who are beyond our control, the fear of people who worship a different god, the fear of being rejected by God, the fear of hell that compels us to believe absolutely because our life depends on it. Only if we can somehow demonstrate that we are holy and loyal and worthy of God's protection and God's affirmation, can we ultimately feel safe and secure.

The most common form of religion, which is based in this rhetoric of fear, is political and radical fundamentalism. Radical fundamentalism is alive and well in each of the world's major religions, and it is a peculiarly dangerous form of faith. Fundamentalists cannot feel safe unless they are convinced, without a shadow of a doubt, that their way to God is the only way. Consequently, their most passionate belief and the point about which they must argue to the end is that, for example in the case of Christianity, there is "no other name" by which one can approach God except Jesus. If there is any other means of achieving the affirmation of God, their faith is shattered. Absolute exclusivity becomes the first principle of belief.

When you set Christian exclusivity over against Islamic or Jewish exclusivity, conflict inevitably arises. War becomes a religious obligation. Sometimes war takes the less fatal, but equally deadly, form of rejection and condemnation. In other cases, war is fought with poison and missiles. In each case, people kill and maim both physically and psychologically in the name of God. The Presbyterian minister who sits today in a federal prison because he killed a physician who performed abortions says, years after his conviction, that "I know that I did the right thing," and that he was obligated by God to kill the physician. The spiritual journey which led him to this conclusion and such a murderous act is rather akin to the spiritual journey of Osama bin Laden. They are both children of an evil religion, a religion that has been formed of fear and retribution rather than grace and freedom.

For many people, the only escape from the bondage of an evil, perverted, and twisted form of religious devotion is to move toward a radical secularism. Countless individuals have never experienced, or even observed, healthy religious devotion and conduct. As a result, in order to break through the constraints of bad religion, a person chooses to abandon religion and religious institutions altogether. We are left, in those cases, with a society of individuals who have no religious moorings which they trust. They adopt some sort of "civil religion" which embraces commonly accepted standards of human behavior, enabling people to live together in reasonable harmony and respect. For thousands of people in the world, even millions, no religion has become a better and more moral option than bad religion.

At their wellsprings, Judaism, Christianity, and Islam are kindred religions. They honor the same prophets and hold many tenets in common. We should be clear that their commonality should not diminish their distinctiveness. Each of the world's faiths brings a distinct vision of God and, it may be argued, each faith bears some special light from God. The notion that, as a follower of Jesus, one has to deny that any person has any light from God by any other means is simply arrogant and unnecessary nonsense.

People with healthy religious perspectives and genuine religious devotion need to find new and persistent ways of engaging in conversations with persons of other faiths in order to seek mutual understanding and to achieve a greater appreciation for one another and for one another's beliefs. No human religion possesses a perfect understanding of God. While God's light may indeed be clear and perfect, the human perception and understanding of God will always be flawed. The highest instincts of the major world religions point toward the ultimate reality of grace and love. God's affirmation of humanity is not an end to be achieved but a gift to set people free.

Violent religion, in all of its forms, is one of the tragedies from which religion and mankind need to be delivered. Muslims around the world want to see their faith rescued from the hands of militant and violent Islamic fundamentalists. They know, as do we, that the hope of faith does not rest in human rejection and violence. The hope of faith rests in learning to live together with the strength to love and the grace to embrace one another and to live together in human community with respect and civility.

Violence in the name of faith should bring us to a new understanding of the value and the urgency of higher learning. Facing into this confluence of terrorism and religion, we begin to see more clearly the genuine sacredness of the work of teaching and learning. In a world that is being torn and crippled by terrorism, the work of teaching and learning takes on a profoundly new significance. These times should teach us that thought should not be made solely the servant of belief. Thought must remain independent, and the commitment to reason must remain unencumbered. The search for justice and human civility should not become the mere step-child of religious belief. While religious belief will often shape our behavior and our values, the hope of human civilization also rests in our ability to bring reason and respect to the table where difficult choices must be made and where complex problems must be solved.

We should remember that human civilization is yet in its infancy. We have made great strides in the past few thousand years. But, in reality, all peoples have not advanced at the same pace. The presence of large human pockets of ignorance and poverty in the world poses a deadly serious threat to the progress of civilization. Fundamentalism preys upon these pockets of ignorance and poverty. As a result, it is altogether possible for the human race to disintegrate in the dust and the fumes of war and terrorism. Our destiny as a civilization is not at all clear and certain. Our destiny is clouded by the ascendancy of violence in the name of God, letting loose irrational and powerful forces of conflict.

Preachments will not alone solve our human dilemma. Pious admonitions can inspire and, perhaps, they may convert us to a higher understanding of God. But delivering religious rhetoric will not be enough to save our civilization. Faith must be joined with reason. Believing must be conditioned by thinking.

We must become learners again. Hope lies in learning, and the work of learning and teaching has never been a more compelling calling. If we are to find hope, we must unite faith and reason, learning and believing, in order to find a better way. We must discover new ways to solve old problems. We must learn to respect people who meet us with different ideas and values and who live by different meanings. We must learn to reason together.

The University is a sanctuary of learning. We are more about learning than teaching, more about nurturing the spirit than delivering right religious doctrine. The future of human civilization may well depend on our ability both to engage the work of teaching and learning and the work of fostering a faith that is open and tolerant.

In the final analysis, in a world that is battered by terrorism and war, our high calling as a university is to become an engine for human hope by calling one another to a life of reason and justice. Our highest work is to educate a new generation who will bring creative and imaginative solutions to problems such as violence and poverty that our present generation has left unsolved. And when we act out that higher calling of teaching and learning, of thinking and believing, we can cross a boundary into a new land of promise. We can move nearer to becoming thoughtful and caring people of grace whose most important legacy will be helping a new generation to take new and bolder steps toward achieving a more civilized world where the human spirit is nurtured by both faith and reason.

2

Becoming a Holy Nation in the Face of a Holy War*

You and I are not defined by the passing of days, of hours or minutes, or even of months or years. The truth is that our lives can never quite be summed up by the days we live. Moments turn out to be more important than minutes. In each of our histories, it is the moments that count, not the minutes. There are moments that are unique and defining for each of us— some experience, some encounter, some event that makes an indelible difference. There are moments in your life which no other individual shares and which alter forever the contours of your life. Think about it. When certain, specific events occur, we are never quite the same. These special moments in your life are sometimes public. Often they are private. An encounter, a marriage, a divorce, an automobile accident, an illness, a fire, an angry word, a broken relationship, an enduring friendship.

There perhaps have been, or certainly there will be, moments that define your professional lives—a choice between duty and devotion, a choice between money and integrity, a choice between doing the right thing and doing what will get you by. The people you meet, the cases you

---

*These remarks were delivered at the Walter F. George School of Law on September 11, 2002, on the occasion of joining in a national day of remembrance on the one-year anniversary of "9/11."

argue, the decisions you make will make their mark on you. They will alter the steps you take as a professional.

But, beyond moments that define our personal lives and our professional lives, there are moments that define our lives together, our corporate lives, our lives as citizens of a nation, and our lives as citizens of the world.

We have drawn aside today, September 11, 2002, because we cannot escape the presence of September 11, 2001. This day on the calendar will not be the same. This morning at 8:46, the bells on the main campus of the University pealed as we observed a moment of silence on our campuses and joined hands with people around our nation.

September 11, or 9/11 as we have come to call it, has become a watermark for America, imprinted indelibly, though not always visibly, upon everything we do. This startling moment, this moment in which we all fell silent, has changed our nation forever. We are unlikely to ever cross the threshold of this day on our calendar without being distracted from the ordinary.

Clearly, we have become a nation far more aware of our vulnerability. Before September 11, we would not have been preoccupied with the regimens or the rhetoric of homeland security. I yet remember a sense of feeling vulnerable during the Cold War in the 1960s. People were building bomb shelters in their homes. After September 11, there seems no place to run, no safe shelter.

In the aftermath and the bewilderment of watching towers crumble and a tragedy that caused us all to weep, we recovered among us a sense of healthy patriotism, rescuing for a time that great tradition, wrenching it away from the crazies, the self-appointed militia living in the wilderness, and the unbridled right-wingers who were stealing and defiling the notion of being a patriot.

As we remember this dreadful, defining moment, we should learn that we will be tempted to take away the wrong lessons from September 11. This day bears searing, unforgettable testimony that we have not yet become fully civilized. At best we are somewhere along the way of becoming civil people, perhaps only in the infancy of that long journey. This anguishing event and its twisted wreckage expose the deep divides and the profound suspicions that haunt us along our way of trying to become more human. We are stunned by the hatred and bitterness that yields such destructive passion. Whenever people act hatefully and cruelly in the name of God or in the name of Allah, it is usually because they are acting in inhuman ways. Fear drives us toward hatred, and we claim the approval of God in order to dampen the guilt that floods in from our own conscience.

Coping with our own raw sense of vulnerability, we are tempted to become focused on some combination of "buttoning-up" and revenge. We are naturally inclined to strengthen barriers, to build walls, to secure boundaries. We find ourselves becoming a more closed society. Our reactions, mine and yours, are born of grief and dismay, born of fear and moral indignation, all of which are lodged deep within us. And while we have now engaged and are likely to remain engaged for years to come in this war against terrorism, we should not ourselves fall prey to regarding such actions as our own holy war. The war against terrorism is not a holy war. The acts of Al-Qaeda do not constitute a holy war. A war against Iraq would not be a holy war. These wars may represent the best that we can do, the best we can muster as a nation. But we would be mistaken to believe that our ultimate victory will be wrought by our military might. Wars, at best, represent our efforts to protect the modest advancements of civilization, but they will rarely, if ever, become themselves instruments for advancing the progress of civilization.

Our human hope will lie in other directions. In the final analysis, becoming more closed, securing our boundaries will not bring us hope. At most, these steps can only deter tragedy. Intolerance and prejudice against other true believers who are themselves victims of the "holy war syndrome" will not bring us hope. We will have to look elsewhere if we are to find hope for our civilization.

Let us learn this hard lesson: Hatred cannot drive out hatred. Intolerance and prejudice cannot overcome ignorance and hostility. So, our day of remembrance will itself become defiled if we use our mourning to whip up the fires of national hostility and revenge.

Let our day of remembrance be marked more by silence than by scorching rhetoric. In truth, the pathway of light and the way that breeds human hope is close to where you live and near the heart of what you study and teach here. Military power may hold off the defeat of civilization's gains, but military power alone can never yield civilization's promise.

Human hope will have a chance when we hold high the canons of justice and the gifts of grace. "Justice" and "grace" seem frail words in the face of crumbling towers and fallen heroes. But let us learn this lesson—a lesson more to live than to speak. The courage to pursue justice and the courage to embody grace will give us light that will never come from the blazing light of bombs and bullets. The relentless pursuit of justice and learning to live with grace will be the lamps of light that bring us hope.

Our life together must reach for a wider embrace. Let us remember: God is not a Christian. God is not a Muslim. And God is not a Jew. God is above all our little gods. God is *with* us all. God is *in* us all. God is *for* us all.

The tragedy of human evil is that in our fear, our human insecurity, we cannot find a way to be present in the world for one another. It will take great courage to pursue justice and to embody grace, ultimately far more courage than to bear weapons. But I believe it is the only way to become a civilized people.

Pursue justice. Live with grace. On that pathway, we can become the people of God and a holy nation.

3

Toxic Ideas
and the Role of the University

During times of national and international peril, the role of the university is not simply to provide an eloquent rationale for the American way. Our democratic structures remain, I believe, civilization's greatest social triumph, but even these structures, which we treasure so deeply, will not be civilization's last triumph. The university has an even higher calling—to engage the world of ideas, to shape and ignite the thoughts that bring humanity to yet greater achievements. The university has a responsibility to become a powerful, unrelenting voice for overcoming the emergence of toxic ideas among humankind. The devotion to wrong ideas and wrong thinking disrupts and often sets back the human journey toward civility and justice.

Three values must, in my view, be held high as priorities if we are to realize the highest and best meaning of being a university. They are *freedom*, *reason*, and *grace*. The sinister emergence of wrong ideas in the world cannot withstand the light and power of freedom, and reason, and grace. And, these values underlie the resilience and energy of liberal education.

Liberal learning remains first and foremost about broadening our understanding of what it means to be fully present and fully human. The need for learning, for open inquiry, has rarely been more urgent. Our being present in this time and at this place is a gift, but that gift can be diminished by the corrosive power of wrong, toxic ideas that we are expected to accept without thought or question. Toxic ideas paralyze the mind and their consequences hobble the progress of human civilization.

We are all plagued by the diseases of fear and insecurity, and most of our toxic ideas arise from this dark side of our human experience. Because we are limited in our sight and thought, limited by the contours of place and time, limited by the unnerving presence of other people whose inner thoughts and motivations we cannot fathom, we build protective fences and defensive mechanisms for managing our fears. These powerful defensives often become transformed into deadly and dehumanizing ideas that drive hostile and violent actions, crippling human relationships.

Certain clues leap out as sure signs of the presence of toxic ideas. Intolerance, for example, is a clue that our thoughts have been captured by fear. Neither persons nor ideas should prevail by force or intimidation. Intolerance often reflects the refusal to confront different ideas and different values on their merits. However, valuing tolerance over intolerance does not mean that anything goes. Tolerance means that, while there may be limits on human actions and behavior, those limits do not automatically apply to thought and ideas. The most devilish of ideas should be debated and, indeed, disarmed by reason and the light of rational discourse. The path to enlightened thinking is not to deny the worth of the wrong thinker. It is to demonstrate through reason and discourse a better way. So, our intolerance of toxic ideas should not come by denouncing them, but by exposing them to the light of debate and reason.

Intolerance is akin to prejudice—another symptom of toxic ideas. The life of prejudice, to which we have all fallen victim, male and female, black and white, gay and straight, is a condition of placing the accidental above the essential. None of us chooses to be born male or female, minority or majority, American or Asian. Yet, these "accidental" conditions of birth frequently become measures for competence and worth. The work of prejudice is to place the accidental above the essential, to decide what a person knows, or what a person can do, or what a person is worth on the basis of the accidental characteristics of his or her being present in the world. It is a pernicious, yet persistent, characteristic of toxic ideas.

Toxic ideas are also characterized by the urge to control and to manipulate. Control is a prominent human means of coping with fear and insecurity. Relating to other people through control springs from viewing another person and his or her way of life as a threat to the stability of our own.

In brief, toxic ideas are ideas that breed hostility, control, intolerance, generating a destructive way of being in the world. Terrorism, for example, is bred by toxic ideas. The intifada among some Palestinians exemplifies the consequences of toxic ideas. People whose minds and spirits are consumed by revenge, the determination to control or destroy at any price, are victims of the power of wrong ideas.

Totalitarianism in any of its forms is an example of a toxic, destructive idea. In a communist system, or a system of government based on totalitarian ideas, the leader uses his power to control and dominate and even terrorize his followers rather than protect and advance their interests. It is a system that turns a human being into an object of manipulation and abuse. Any social system that presumes to know what is best for its participants and proceeds to impose the "best" is simply a form of unbridled authoritarianism.

Strangely enough, this form of social ordering is far more prevalent than we might wish to believe. We today easily reject and look with horror on such visible forms as Stalinist Communism and Hitler's Nazism. The world community sits in judgment on the tyranny of Slobadan Milosevic. Yet, day after day, we find comfort in discarding our freedom to think independently. In reality, the masses of people who concede to unconditional authority are not required to do so. It is a safer, more convenient way to deal with their uncertainties. Whatever its liabilities, the appeal of unconditional authority is the sense of certainty it bestows. Rarely are our freedom and our independence torn away from us. We more often eagerly turn ourselves over to the power of another.

While political totalitarianism is rapidly going out of vogue, despotism in business, politics, and religion continues to abound. Corporations abusing employees for the rewards of the few; relatively open governments that control the public will through fear and intimidation; fundamentalist preachers who prescribe the *only* safe and secure way to gain God's approval, are ugly and destructive forms of despotic behavior.

Moral relativism and moral absolution are both toxic ideas. The notion that anything goes or that every person should do what feels good is a destructive idea. Every person's moral choice must be bounded by personal integrity and social responsibility. But the real alternative to relativism is not a moral absolutism where every action can responsibly be characterized as good or evil in advance. Context and intent and results do have a bearing on moral value. So, one part of the journey of learning is to free us from the false dichotomies that are set forth to control our lives. It requires more courage and integrity to be fully present with the deep and difficult conflicts of life and to make judgments that lay claim to reason and compassion in order to decide what is the right thing to do.

Destructive ideas can be quite subtle. The idea that death is our worst or our ultimate enemy is, in my judgment, a toxic idea. Life is not first and foremost about staying alive. Life is far more about finding meaning for our being here. The mere addition of days will not add life. It will, at most, only delay death. The investments we make in delaying death are important and usually responsible commitments to improving life. They are sometimes irresponsible because death is not our worst enemy. On countless occasions, death should and can be embraced as a friend.

The rise of ideas that diminish what it means to be human will continue to arise in every human arena. The debate about human cloning has only begun. Finding responsible outcomes for the debates will require more than science and legislation. It will require wisdom. The defenders of cloning are not wittingly friends of evil. They want to preserve cloning as a human option for exercising people's right to have children with "desirable genes." And, there will almost certainly within the century be cloning of human organs that will cure diseases and restore health to the formerly incurable.

Opponents responsibly argue that human cloning is a dangerous and slippery slope, leading to children by design. State and federal legislation has been introduced and, in some places, enacted to ban human cloning. But such legislative remedies will not alone be sufficient. The human conscience must struggle with these issues of whether human cloning represents a profound defilement of our essential human nature and a radical form of child abuse. Or, does human cloning, now in its most nascent and primitive stages, represent the coming stages of human evolution? The answers will require more than pontifical pronouncements. They will require our common human struggle with the meaning of our being here. Is human cloning a toxic idea or precursor of a new stage of human evolution? Our answers will require the wisdom that can flow only from thought and compassion.

This University operates in a world of ideas, ideas that can make us more civil and enlightened, as well as ideas that can diminish and destroy. Our work and our challenge as a university, is to create and sustain an educational program that provides intellectual capital and a stable context for nurturing the human spirit. The work of the University is to enable individuals to think imaginatively and critically about the complex issues of being alive in the world today.

The university experience is first and foremost about finding our own vocation to think and to speak about the difficult and disturbing issues that confront us. We must, indeed, enlarge our students' capacities for competence and for professional service. But achieving competence alone will not be enough. Addressing the largest and most challenging issues faced by our students, by the families they produce, and by the societies they build will require more than professional discipline and competence. Meeting the challenges will require careful, disciplined thought and a commitment to compassion. Our educational experience should enable students to become thoughtful and caring citizens, who lead our human order to a new horizon of seeing the highest and best hope that lies within us. We have to be concerned with setting people free from ideas that destroy and diminish, providing them with the intellectual capacity and the spiritual maturation to make wise human choices.

Now, to return to my opening thesis. The achievement of an education that leads to engaging our lives and our relationships with thought and compassion will require, I believe, at least three underlying values and priorities—values that might be called antidotes for toxic ideas. They are freedom, reason, and grace.

Intellectual freedom and the independence of thought lie at the center of a liberal education—an education that liberates. Controlling thought and manipulating human opinion are the antithesis of a liberal education. Imposing rigid doctrinal precepts and passing them off as education denies the essence of liberal learning. Intellectual freedom carries risks, but those risks must be embraced if we are to genuinely nurture the human spirit. We cannot do our work as a university unless we are devoted to the canons of intellectual freedom and academic independence. Faculty must be protected to study and to teach even when we think they may be wrong. The open pursuit and debate of ideas cannot be dismantled because those ideas annoy certain constituencies of the university. A critical role of administrators, especially chief administrators, is to protect and to preserve the open pursuit of learning wherever the search leads and whomever the search offends.

The second requirement, if we are to do the good work of a university, is our devotion to reason. If we are to overcome the barriers of prejudice and intolerance, it will be through our common commitment to the power of reason.

Our appeals to reason are not flawless. Unfortunately, some individuals manage to make persuasive cases in support of the irrational. So, our pursuit of the rational must be subjected to the refining fires of debate and dialogue. While our logic and our reason are fallible, they remain our principal agents for combating the presence of toxic ideas. The university must hold high the power of reason as the highest and best means of achieving and maintaining respect, civility, and justice.

The third priority is to help people become more fully human, to help them learn to live with grace. Grace is life's most important gift. Without grace our lives become hollow and empty. Reason and freedom combined will not by themselves bring us hope.

Grace is far more a human word than a religious word. Grace is a word about how persons connect with one another. Grace recognizes the essential worth of every person and acknowledges every person as a bearer of certain, specific talents and gifts in the world. Grace enables us to lay claim to the value of another person, discovering that we cannot be whole in isolation. It is grace that enables us to see beyond the boundaries and barriers that separate us and to see in another person the completion and fulfillment of our own presence in the world. So, grace is not simply the altruism of selfless caring, although every act of caring is an act of grace. Grace is the way of light that enables us ultimately to know ourselves. It is through meeting and connecting that we know ourselves most fully. Otherwise, we remain mere fragments of humanity, trying to survive until we die.

In a sense, grace is the culmination of freedom and reason. Without freedom, we cannot grow. Without reason, we cannot sustain life. Without grace, we cannot fulfill our lives.

These priorities provide the foundation for overcoming the power of toxic ideas and grasping the power of becoming a thoughtful, compassionate person. Evil indeed abounds. The presence of terrorism, of social and political totalitarianism, of religious fundamentalism that saps the energy and integrity of all the world's faiths are all products of wrong ideas.

The burden and calling of the university is both to teach and to embody a better way of being in the world. Our calling is high. Our work is holy. If we are to sustain the advance of civilization, we must sustain the gift of learning, and sustaining that gift will become a wellspring of hope and light for the world in which we live.

4

The Courage Factor

We were recently stunned, caught up in an inexorable sense of national sadness, over the loss of the *Columbia* with its crew of six Americans and one Israeli. These men and women were hailed as heroes, an accolade that flowed genuinely from our national sense of grief, as well as our sense of being indebted to these young, gifted men and women who literally gave their lives in the service of learning and exploration.

In the aftermath of the *Columbia* tragedy, I sent the following message to the University community.

> The University community joins our nation and the world in mourning the tragic loss of the *Columbia* with its crew of six Americans and one Israeli. These gifted individuals were partners with us in the great enterprise of learning. While working in different and daring environs, they like all men and women of thought and deliberation were pushing back the boundaries of ignorance and bringing new knowledge and understanding to humankind, helping to make possible the continuing progress of civilization. As colleagues of research, teaching, discovery, and learning, we salute the work and the courage of these seven astronauts who gave their lives in the noble service of learning and the advancement of human civilization. May God be with them and with us.

The loss of the *Columbia* will lead to what will inevitably seem like interminable inquiries into the causes of the *Columbia* tragedy and systems revisions that will seek to make our explorations of space a little safer. Yet, no amount of systems improvement will ever displace the courage factor that lies within the psyche of every astronaut and which, I believe, lies hidden deep within the soul of every person who chooses research and teaching as a mission for life.

While most teachers or researchers do not place their personal lives in grave jeopardy in their daily work, the decision to confront the world's ignorance and prejudice with the awesome power of inquiry and intellectual freedom always requires the courage factor. There are no risk-free environments for learning, and every experience of genuine learning poses a challenge to what we believe to be true.

Teaching and learning carries with it the nascent courage to confess our ignorance. The philosopher Socrates identified knowledge with virtue, affirming that the foundation for *doing* what is good is *knowing* what is good. Socrates would have taught us that ignorance is the root of the human travail. To the importance of knowing, Aristotle added that the yearning to know is intrinsic to our being human, that is, that all people by nature desire to know. And while the astronaut and the poet have chosen different modes of learning, they are both exploring the deep recesses of human understanding and probing the meaning of our common human experience.

The yearning for knowledge and understanding lies deep within all of us. While none of us ever escapes the yearning, we can allow our lives to be consumed by mindless distractions that range from the safe haven of a drug-enhanced numbness to coping with our world through the monotony of work that does not bring joy or purpose, or the increasingly empty theatrics of "reality" television.

Confronting our own ignorance requires enormous courage. If anything is more prominent in our lives than the yearning to know, it may be the pretense of knowing. Our pretentious understanding is often loud with sounds of certainty and characteristically replaces courage with bravado. So, while we long to know, we find it very difficult to confess that we do not know.

The lack of knowledge, much less its confession, is felt as the lack of power and the loss of power always seems to threaten our foundations. But what brings the University together is never that we have achieved and possess the power of knowledge. To the contrary, the University is a community of learners who have the courage to confess that our knowledge is profoundly limited and our understanding has only begun. We are in the infancy of human understanding. Of all places, the University should be a place where humility and respect for differences prevails over intellectual arrogance.

In the face of the great inner and outer mysteries that face mankind, I believe the confession of ignorance is the first and most important foundation of learning. Of course, ignorance should not be confused with skepticism. Skepticism doubts whether we can know; ignorance acknowledges that we do not yet know fully. Skepticism tends to be arrogant and unbending—aloof and disenchanted by the search for truth.

So, the pretense of possessing knowledge is among the greatest deterrents to learning. We are inclined to become enamored with our own ideas and judgments. We like to speak with authority and absoluteness. In the Academy the most important moments are likely not those marked by an avalanche of words, but the moments of silence that interrupt our rapid rhetoric. For the teacher, it is the silence of listening and thinking, the silence of pondering and reflection that enable that teacher to move from stammering assertions to eloquent insight. When we walk within the University or before our students as masters of knowledge, we veil only thinly that we are servants of ignorance. Our teaching is rarely grounded in limitless reservoirs of knowledge. The best teachers inevitably are those who themselves are actively and vigorously engaged in learning. Learning leaves us open and tentative, listening and stretching to see into a new crevice of truth. Learning enables us to be surprised by the unexpected breaking of new light while trampling through the forests of darkness.

Universities will not succeed in ridding the world of all ignorance. Our calling is more modest. The hope we give will be more likely in fostering the courage to walk or to fly into the mystery boldly, to push back the boundaries of inner space and outer space in order that we all may live more fully as children of light. We salute our fellow learners, the seven courageous men and women of the *Columbia* who gave their lives in our common quest to push back the boundaries of ignorance. In their life and death, they embodied the highest instincts of the human spirit, and they remind us all that there will be no learning apart from the courage factor.

5

Women in the Twenty-First Century

We can celebrate it, be dismayed by it, but we should not ignore this reality: the twenty-first century will be the century of the woman. For starters, there are more women than men in the world—not because more women than men are born. The fact is that girl babies survive at a higher rate than boys, and then they live longer than men. Women are a stronger breed.

But numbers are not the whole story. We have learned that, on average, women are smarter. They are better learners, better managers, and better educated than men. In K-12, boys have been four times more likely to drop out of school than girls. More women go to college than men. If the present trend continues at our public universities, the only men on campus will be the football team. The more selective colleges and universities become, the more difficult it becomes to maintain strong male enrollments.

But let me be a little more precise about women's abilities. When I say that women are brighter than men, what I am really saying is that the bell curve is tighter for women than for men. There are actually more men in the world who are geniuses, but there are also a lot more stupid people who are men.

In 1970, there were about 400,000 businesses owned by women. But the big story, which made the cover of *Fortune* magazine, was about the fifty most powerful women in American business. Women now own more than ten million businesses. These companies post over 2.5 trillion dollars in sales, and they employ more than twenty million people. More than half of the jobs created in this country in the last decade have been created by women-owned businesses. In addition, more than fifteen million women earn more than their spouses, and that number is rising fast.

Women today account for 3.5 trillion dollars in consumer and commercial spending every year. At least forty-five percent of Americans with assets of more than $500,000 are women. Women make three out of four healthcare decisions. Women spend two out of three healthcare dollars. Women make sixty-five percent of the car-buying decisions. Only ten percent of the automobile salespersons are women. That will change. But the car companies are getting it. Only a few years ago, Ford aimed more than sixty percent of their magazine ads at men. They are now aiming more than sixty percent at women.

In 1979, one percent of the business travelers were women. Today, women do more than fifty percent of the business travel. And, the hotels are getting it. They are focusing more on women travelers. New amenities have been introduced, including full-length mirrors, hair dryers, irons, and ironing boards. But, of greater importance, a change in the culture of training employees that may be summarized this way: Show women guests respect! The CEO of one major hotel chain has instructed his employees not to assume that the man is always paying the bill. Hotels are getting it.

In management, a recent two-year study included 941 managers (672 men and 269 women) from more than 200 organizations. The evaluation scheme is what is commonly called 360 degree feedback—that is, managers were rated by subordinates, bosses, and peers in twenty categories. In fifteen of the twenty categories, women were rated better managers, especially in planning, setting standards, and decisiveness.

But, more important than these numbers is to begin to unravel some of the differences in styles of management. Men focus more on separation. Women focus more on connection. Men often measure success by the degree of separation—how many people are between them and their subordinates. A large office on the top floor of a fifty-floor tower is seen as a sign of success despite the fact that the boss is removed from the people that he leads. On the other hand, women are inclined to be closer to their subordinates, reaching out, not reaching down—touching, nurturing. Authority among women leaders is more likely to come from connection to, rather than distance from. Women are more into networks, less into hierarchies. Men tend to be more exclusive, women more inclusive. So, it is no surprise that men tend to solve problems with confrontation. Women are more likely to emphasize finding common ground.

In the professions these small differences are beginning to show up in big ways. A decade ago, very little was heard in the law profession of dispute resolution and mediation. Today alternative dispute resolution is a prominent part of the legal system, and that development just happens to coincide with the fact that more than half of the new law students are women. Women will change the practice of law from the codification of conflict to the codification of cooperation. More than half of the students admitted to the Yale School of Medicine, and about half of the students admitted to Mercer's Medical School here in a Deep South city, are women. As a result, the practice of medicine will undergo radical revision—a shift from conquering disease, a control orientation, to fostering health, a relationship orientation.

The signs of a new century are unmistakable. In reality, of course, we are not talking about male versus female. The issue before us is not whether we can invert the hierarchy, that is, move from a patriarchal formula to a matriarchal formula. The fundamental issue is not who will be in charge. Even so, we can be sure of this fact. By the middle—not the end—of this century, at least half of Fortune 500 companies will have women CEOs. The reason has nothing to do with the Equal Rights Amendment or even laws regarding gender equity. The matter is more straightforward. No corporation can exclude half of the talent pool and expect to remain competitive. Women will prevail in the free-market system because they are smarter, and they are becoming better educated. More than half of the best talent over the next fifty years will be female. More than half of the bachelors and masters degrees will go to women. Competitive companies will claim that talent. "Yes, sir!" will give way to "Yes, ma'am!"

A new century is upon us, and very elementary structural changes are taking place in how society, corporations, and institutions work. I want to identify briefly five systemic changes, which I believe will change the workplace and the social interaction on which we base our lives. These are lessons that if we have the will to see and the courage to learn will enable us to become more effective, more productive, and ultimately more civilized.

When you think about it, the human race is a young and recent development in the world order. If the entire development of our cosmos were viewed as a twenty-four-hour period, humans would have existed less than a second. We are a recent occurrence. We are still thrashing around in partial chaos, learning our way and charting the human course.

The philosopher Plato said, "Civilization is the victory of persuasion over force." We have embarked on the pathway toward civilization. Yet we live much of our lives, and our nation's lives, by exercising force, prescribing brutality, and embellishing power. So, I offer you five truths that I believe will redefine the twenty-first century.

1. *Cooperation will prevail over coercion.* We have all known circumstances when nothing would serve to work except force. You draw clear boundaries for children. "Do not play in the street." Boundaries are ways of surviving, so that we can grow up. The problem is that some of us survive, but never grow up. And a failed "growing up" is when a person continues to live by exercising or being the object of coercion—by hitting or being hit, by controlling or being controlled, by placing others in bondage or being placed in a prison of their own. The life of coercion, whether one is controlling or being controlled, is the lowest rung on the ladder of civilization. It is barely the first step on our climb out of the slime.

The twenty-first century will witness the struggle to overcome the politics of coercion, and that journey will, in part, be driven by the rise of women's leadership.

Whenever coercion is required—and surely on some occasions nothing else will seem to serve the situation—it probably means that we have managed poorly. The urge to dominate, to rule, to exercise rigorous control more often reflects the needs of the manager, the leader, than the require-ments of the health of the organization. Khomeini's Iran, Hitler's Germany, Saddam Hussein's Iraq, and Stalin's Soviet Union had striking similarities. They were all characterized by a rigid male dominance.

But the signs are clear. We are moving toward more decentralized structures, less top-down command, nurturing rather than coercion, more win-win, less win-lose approaches to solving problems. We are moving, in short, toward a different architecture of human interaction. And this new architecture will redefine the workplace and the ways in which men and women relate to one another. Women will exercise responsibilities heretofore reserved for men and men will embrace values that heretofore have been regarded as soft and feminine, more relational, less hierarchical. It is a part of our quiet, but important journey toward a higher civilization.

2. *The power of analysis will be conditioned and enriched by the power of intuition.* Intuition is not a women's trait. Intuition is a critical human capacity, which has been diminished and hidden amidst male ascendancy.

Western civilization, far more than Eastern civilization, has been marked by the power of analysis. Analysis is the centerpiece of scientific inquiry. You understand the world by taking it apart. The most compelling analysis with which we have begun the twenty-first century has been the mapping of the human gene pool. This analysis will provide a reservoir of knowledge with which to achieve better health and longer life.

The prevailing science of the twentieth century was physics, and with that science we produced X-rays, atomic weapons, and space shuttles. The prevailing science of the twenty-first century will be biology, and with that science we will develop new human organs and biologically based computers, far more powerful than those based on binary logic, computers that will learn and think, computers that will become partners in the advance of human civilization.

Physics represents the power of analysis. Biology represents the power of synthesis, and synthesis is the hallmark of human intuition. Intuition is a methodology for understanding the part by one's sense of the whole. In today's corporate world, decision making based solely on facts, figures, and hard data will often be too little, too late. Corporate CEOs are learning that intuition is a human capacity worthy to be developed and fostered. It represents the creative capacity to see through the chaos and apprehend a fresh solution.

The surest way to develop intuition is to go more slowly rather than faster. Fear blocks and blinds intuition. So does pressure to perform. Studies of runners have shown that running or jogging produces a rush of endorphins, a pleasurable relaxation response, but when a runner begins training for competition, the flow of endorphins is often blocked. Intuition works best and becomes most reliable in a context where we can listen to the pulse, to the rhythms of relationships. Analysis tends to cut us off from the rhythm of our life and work. Intuition values the rhythm.

3. *Leadership will become more about the power to nurture than the power to control.* Power and authority have been the defining hallmarks of twentieth-century management. Leadership has been equated with power—power to influence, power to control, power to direct, power to create, power to destroy, power to hold, power to let go, power to encumber, power to restrict and to silence, power to set free. The power of control has been the most common expression of leadership.

Former British Prime Minister Margaret Thatcher, so often thought of as a woman who exemplifies male values, gave wonderful expression to her female sense of strategy when asked how she had attained her success. She said, "I have never spelled out specific goals for myself or aspired to a particular position. Rather, I have seized opportunities as they came and made the best of them." Barbara Grogan, an international contractor in Denver, echoed the same theme: "I can't say where I'll be in five years; five years ago I could never have foreseen where I am now. I don't draft five-year plans—I just do the best job I can and trust that it will lead to where I'm supposed to be next. I know that sounds sort of squishy, but it works."

Leadership in the twenty-first century will require an increasing measure of spontaneity and the capacity to nurture more than direct and command.

The corporate conversation is being altered by the larger presence of women and the contours of leadership are being modified by a terrain that is being reshaped by the feminine principle—the principle of nurture. We are all aware that as women have begun to advance in the corporate workplace, they have been expected to embrace a prevailing male model for success—some version of command and control. But much of our difficulty arises from the stereotype itself. The issue is not whether you can get "man" out of management. The issue is that leadership in a new century cannot rely upon a narrow set of human gifts. It is not enough to say that men are rational and women are wise. Leadership will require reason and wisdom, vision and discipline, women and men.

4. *In the twenty-first century, social value and economic value will become bound together inextricably.* People are waking up to the reality that they are responsible for the quality of their lives. Blaming mom and dad for the way we turned out just does not cut it anymore. Similarly, blaming the boss, or the corporation, or the government is pointless and only reinforces an "us versus them" mentality. We are at the stage where, if we are not a part of the solution, we are part of the problem.

We are awakening to new reality everywhere. Here in Macon, Georgia, after complaining of government and politics for years, corporate and lay voices are beginning to take things in their own hands.

In our progress toward becoming civilized and civilizing our organizations, we have to move beyond creating either organizational or economic systems that generate victor and victims. Our success, or even our achievement, of a measure of wealth cannot be built on the shoals of victimizing other people. Our success can never be success if it is built upon human deception or defiling our human or natural environment.

Social value and economic value converge in the realization that we are stewards—stewards of our own talents, stewards of our relationships, and stewards of our physical environment. Whenever human achievement is based upon an abuse of those primary stewardships, the outcome will be destructive and self-defeating. The realization of economic value cannot be achieved without social consequences. This new century is ushering in an era in which economic decisions cannot be reached without a candid and honest inquiry into social outcomes.

The linking of economic and social value, far from being a burden for business, can become itself an economic engine. For example, the extraordinary partnership of Anita and Gordan Roddick has created a company called the Body Shop (located in malls across America) which has become a model for the socially and ecologically sound corporation of the future. According to Anita Roddick, they sell not only "sound products" but "sound values" from human rights and ecological consciousness to the promise of a humanized workplace. They have grown into a multinational, multimillion-dollar business and have become an important force in social change.

5. *The culture of commerce is being reshaped by an ethos of civility.* Caring about civility should not be confused with a superficial, syrupy sentimentality. Caring and civility are based upon the affirmation that every person matters, and the worth of human order is dependent upon ability to mine the gifts which each person brings to the party. There are no ungifted people. Old habits of management require people to

conform to our ways of behaving—to dance to our tune. New leadership encourages them to listen to their own music. We must create new habits of thinking that regards every person to be a creative gift to the world. The strength of our organization is whether we can unlock the treasures embodied in the talents of every person. Everybody counts.

The cornerstone of caring is listening. Listening, while not impossible, is more difficult in hierarchies and flows more naturally in more web-like organizations. It is easier to communicate from the center than from the top. Nancy Badore, who leads the Executive Development Center at Ford Motor Company, has as her mission to get leaders to listen "down the ladder."

Studies in the gender difference in the use of language suggest that men tend to speak far more than women. Furthermore, the study showed that women's listening is different than men's—more intense, more thoughtful, more attentive.

When once I was asked what the greatest lesson I had learned as president of the University, I replied that my greatest lesson was this: More problems are solved by listening than by talking. Men, especially, like to talk. It is one of the maladies of university administration.

Carol Gilligan, who wrote *In a Different Voice* and who transformed some of my thinking in the 1980s said, that "the ability of women to listen is rooted not just in social subordination, but in the substance of their moral concern." Listening is always a relational act. You can speak without relating but you cannot listen without relating. Listening is our most important affirmation of the value of another person.

Creating an ethos of civility means that a corporation's success depends upon its capacity to claim the ideas, the energy, the creativity, and productivity of every person. Everybody matters.

A new century, bringing new opportunities, new para-
digms, new directions that will sweep through our lives and
the organizations we serve. Frankly, some businesses, some
institutions, some churches, some universities will fear the
change—trying with every word and every gesture to hold on
to old ways of believing.

But, our challenge—yours and mine—is not to become
trapped by the way things have been. The real issue will not
be gender. The issue before us is the courage to probe the
richness of the human gift—the courage to combine risk
taking and competition (more often associated with the
masculine) with intuitive insight and nurturing relationships
(more often associated with the feminine).

Civilization cannot achieve a higher order without celebrating the whole range of the human *persona*—masculine
and feminine. Our future and, indeed, our hope, for this new
century does not lie in a model of domination and subservi-
ence. It lies in the willingness to rediscover our interdependence, to celebrate our differences and to claim the hope of
building businesses and societies, and even our own lives,
upon the celebrating promise of the human bond and upon
embracing the diversity of the human spirit.

By being the century of the woman, the twenty-first
century will enable us to move beyond the rhetoric of male
versus female to a higher plane. We can transcend the
language of domination and conflict and see over into a new
land of promise called interdependence and cooperation.

- 6 -
The Freedom to Dissent

The right to disagree and to express our disagreements is a basic right which is fundamental to our society and indispensable to the community of higher education. The exercise of that right should be conducted in a fashion that preserves honesty, integrity, and fairness. That is to say, it is a right which carries within it certain responsibilities for prudence and reason. The right to dissent derives from our commitment to freedom. Even though some dissent may seem to lie outside the boundaries of responsible dissent, it should, within appropriate limits, be tolerated in order to be sure to protect the right of those persons who wish to disagree in a responsible manner. I believe we are wise to err on the side of tolerance of dissent. Our societies are made better and human civilization is advanced because men and women in different cultures and divergent traditions have vigorously voiced competing and conflicting views.

The right to disagree and to voice our disagreements is one of the hallmarks of a free society and of any institution that is committed to free inquiry. Without that right, open inquiry would become compromised in favor of defending the prevailing view of things. In the end, the advance of knowledge itself can become seriously curtailed. An open society is built on the assumption that truth will not be harmed by inquiry, and further, that our understanding and respect for the truth will be enhanced by a willingness to remain open to questions. Open inquiry, then, is the foundation of free dissent in the context of higher education. We should not encumber the intellect or the human spirit from seeking the truth. The absence of those encumbrances implies the ability to disagree with and to object to the received doctrines and the prevailing views of the world.

The unwillingness to permit dissent historically works contrary to the good of society and actually undermines the respect of the truth. The Copernican revolution that literally shook the foundations of the existing understanding of the world and the place of mankind in the universe took place because Copernicus was unwilling to accept a view of the world that experience would not sustain. Regardless of the views we might prefer to hold, the world and our experience of it could be better explained by a different description of reality. Galileo's conviction that the earth was round instead of flat did not spring from a need to disagree but his need to disagree sprang from a review of the evidence provided by his own experience. He had a responsibility to disagree even when he was not accorded the freedom of dissent.

The very nature of education requires that educators boldly hold high this right to dissent. In its absence, the elementary traditions that undergird learning are transgressed and the cause of learning ultimately suffers. Education differs, in this respect, from other private endeavors. A business or corporation may operate, and even successfully so, as a closed system where the principles on which decisions are based and even the decisions themselves are not subject to dissent. One disagrees by disengaging himself or herself from the enterprise. The right to dissent in our society is not automatically carried over into every organization or institution of which we are a part. The rights conferred by various organizations may vary widely but a person does have the ultimate right to disassociate. In the context of higher education, I believe it is different. There, dissent is intrinsic to the search for truth. If we rule out dissent, we are ruling out the possibility for education. The context of learning requires that statements of truth be open to examination and rebuttal, and that where the evidence requires it, disagreement is a responsibility. For a learning environment, a high value must be placed on critical analysis.

The right to dissent does not, of course, validate dissent. In an open society and an institution, such as higher education, that operates as an open system, dissent has a right to be heard and to be judged on the merits of the evidence. A dissenting view that is dominated or characterized by emotional outbursts is generally short-lived. The tolerance of dissent, however, requires permitting even unfounded and superficial dissent to occur. Dissent, like truth itself, must live and die by the virtues of its own evidence and rationality. Irresponsible dissent ultimately dies from the lack of light. Therefore, while we should probably err on the side of tolerance, the right to dissent is not without its limits. Belonging to the essence of the right to dissent is a constellation of responsibilities pertaining to evidence, reason, and civility.

First and foremost, the right to disagree carries with it the responsibility for mutuality of dissent. Reinhold Niebuhr once observed that the trouble with reformers and revolutionaries is that they come to believe that the evils which they oppose exist only in their enemies. We hear a good deal about tolerating dissent, while we sometimes observe considerably less tolerance from those who dissent. It is often difficult for the dissenter to be tolerant, or he or she feels a strong desire to argue the case vehemently and with a forcefulness that will make the opponent appear unequivocally wrong. While patience and tolerance are qualities which an open society is expected to confer upon those who express dissent, their absence is often gently overlooked in those who dissent. Either tolerance and respect is mutual or it is nothing. The responsibility to tolerate cannot be a unilateral responsibility.

Either we behave with tolerance toward those whose views are contrary to our own or we forfeit our right to have our own views heard with respect and tolerance.

In addition to the responsibility for tolerance is the call to reason. The very heart of dissent rests on an appeal to reason. If we ignore reason, we are undermining the very foundation of legitimate dissent. Free societies and open systems are built on the assumption that where freedom is present, reason will generally prevail. Those who disagree with a certain view, but who wish simply to substitute for that view a set of beliefs that bears their own personal commitment should not expect their disagreement to be taken very seriously.

This approach to dissent has been especially disturbing in the recent religious conflicts. Those persons who have been intent, and indeed who have been very successful, in laying hold of the leadership of the religious groups have been doing so not because they claim that their views have the advantages of reason but because their views represent, for them, the higher revelation of God. In brief, we are admonished to accept their views not because reason requires it but because God says their views are right. This appeal to "higher reason" may indeed be the basis of one's dissent from the established view of the world, but such an appeal cannot be debated. The goal of the appeal is commitment or conversion to a point of view and cannot be affected significantly by rational discourse. Responsible dissent in the context of higher education must appeal to reason and the merits of the dissenting perspective should be evaluated on the basis of reason rather than upon rhetoric and emotion or having been "informed" by a higher authority.

Responsible dissent also attends to the claims of experience. Dissent is judged not only by the rigors of reason but by an examination of the evidence. Any dissent that is unwilling to submit the evidence for its views or the observations on which its claims are based hardly warrants significant reflection. Those who dissent have a responsibility to offer a broader or more comprehensive explanation of present experience. Otherwise their claims are merely fanciful and, though perhaps interesting, they have little basis for being taken seriously.

Finally, responsible dissent should take into account the canons of civility. In any open society or organization, it does matter how we treat one another. Dissent should not ignore the worth and the value of persons who hold contrary views. Every debate and every conflict has boundaries within which the conflict occurs. Even wars among nations tend to observe certain conventions of civilization. Debate itself has boundaries of propriety.

Within higher education and the open democratic society, the exercise of dissent should occur within the context of the affirmation of respect. In the absence of respect, arrogance and anger prevail over fairness and reason. Civility is an imperative for the preservation of the right to dissent.

One of the problems of an open society is that it can become paralyzed by its own debates. In our complex world, issues are often confusing and the clear course of reason or good sense may be quite elusive. The role of governance in an open system such as higher education is to preserve the instincts for freedom, while maintaining order sufficient to permit teaching and research to flourish. In addition, we should exercise the sort of flexible authority that tries to insure that we will not become victimized by our own commitment to freedom and open inquiry.

The governance of societies and institutions preserves freedom by setting boundaries within which freedom is to be exercised. Governance makes freedom possible and freedom makes governance necessary. Governance expedites the preservation of the freedom to dissent and enables us not to be crippled by our own disagreements. Responsible governance must devise and protect the means of hearing dissent.

The endgame of debate and dissent is not only listening. It is choosing. Debate can sharpen our judgments but it should not endlessly delay judgment itself. The role of governance lies in preserving the dynamic tension between freedom and authority. Sufficient authority must be present to expedite the exercise of freedom. Our commitment to freedom reminds us always that because authority is fallible, it should be flexible.

Isaiah Berlin wrote:

> Injustice, poverty, slavery, ignorance—these may be cured by reform or revolution. But men do not live only by fighting evils. They live by positive goals, individual and collective, a vast variety of them seldom predictable, at times incompatible. It is from intense preoccupation with these ends, ultimate, incommensurable, . . . more often than not without conscious hope of success, still less of the approbation of official auditors, that the best moments come in the lives of individuals and peoples.[*]

I believe it is important that we live more by our dreams than by our troubles and that we be guided more by our hopes than by our fears. In the long run, it is better to trust the course of debate than to suppress the right to dissent.

---

[*]Berlin, *Four Essays on Liberty* (London and New York: Oxford University Press, 1969).

The Genius of the University

You and I live in an era in which there is much talk about education. However, respect for education is no longer automatic. And it should not be. Where education has become nothing more than a turnstile to adulthood, it deserves little respect. Even where respect for education remains, it is often accompanied by uneasiness. We are unsure what we should be calling upon our schools to do. Too many people are dropping out. People graduate from high schools without being able to write a cogent paragraph. The schools have come to be expected to serve as social agencies. Schools are called upon to deal with children having children, to cope with guns in the classroom, requiring people to enter schools through entrances decked with metal detectors. People are worried about the state of education.

And on every corner someone has a cure. One school board member fought to eliminate twenty-four books from the curriculum. It is a case of the schools advocating ignorance. Or we look to the lottery for a cure. We figure people can't restrain their urge to take the big gamble so we might as well use it for education. The governor has a cure. The president has a cure. Everyone is troubled. And my guess is that government will not ultimately be able to solve our problem or alleviate our troubles. Government has rarely turned out to be a good parent or a reliable "Big Brother." Governments can be a resource but they can never displace or substitute for an informed and responsible citizenry.

I have wondered how we, as leaders of higher education, fit into the travails of education. Where do we stand?

Last year, I was rather taken by the then recently published papal encyclical entitled *The Splendor of Truth*. And at the risk of sounding unauthentic or even preachy, I want to explore the prospect of recovering some element of moral imperative in our own work of education. Our universities should be institutions with distinctive missions. Do people believe in what they are doing any longer?

By moral imperative, I certainly do not simply have reference to some requirement of religion in the curriculum. Indeed religion may be the source of a lot of our immorality. Religion does too often become the instrument of oppression, fostering submission to a host of external authorities—whether they be husbands or fundamentalist preachers.

The gift of moral discernment is quite another matter—to gain insight, to see beyond the façade of our culture and our busy lives. What is there in the world worth giving ourselves to?

The calling of education should be, in part, to connect excellence and rigor with sanity and prudence—to impart within the young and old who study here a quiet longing for truth and to build up within them the civic courage to link the power of knowledge with the power to act and to make a rational and lasting difference in whatever setting they think and act and make decisions.

Even in a democratic society, the combining of language and technology can enslave as well as set us free. The media, particularly television and radio, combine language and technology in powerful ways. That combination has the power to set us free or to bind us into motionless lockstep. The spate of television commercials during every election campaign season becomes almost surreal. The abuse of language and technology is a far greater threat to our democratic survival than X-rated language or R-rated movies. X-rated language is meant to startle. The language of political advertisement is meant to possess—to take possession of our minds and hearts and souls.

So, the moral dimension of education is hardly the rescue of prayer for the public schools or insuring that every graduate knows the Ten Commandments—though the latter might be an interesting inquiry.

I mean by the recovery of the moral imperative something quite different. I mean to come to terms with the power, the might of human freedom and human judgment, the power to be a person, making a difference for civility and courage, both in the world of industry, professions, and our civil life together, within nations, and within precincts where persons more than politics will determine the quality and the outcome of living together in clusters we call towns and cities.

Education is about laying claim to the human promise, getting in touch with our own highest and best gifts. It is not enough in today's world to educate an engineer or a physician or a teacher who is competent. If we do not do that, we really have no reason to exist and we certainly do not deserve the tuition we receive. But can we do more?

I say that we can and that we should. Our genius should be to loose the shackles that have been so carefully crafted by our society and foster within those who study here the courage and the will to be free people, people who discover their own worth, who revive their own self-respect, and who trust their own ideas. We must educate thinking men and women who dare to make judgments that challenge old commitments and dismantle outworn alliances. All of this is to say that civilizations have to be reborn with every new generation. Our task is to give people the intellectual and moral tools to reshape civilization. It is not enough to sustain our mores and to prop up the structures of society. Their weight will be too great. They will crumble.

I do not worry that our ideas and our civilization may disappear. I worry only about whether we are equipping our young folk to build a better place, to succeed us with better ideas, and it will not be done unless they grasp the promise of their being here. It is a matter of realizing that we are not there yet and that our culture will stall out unless there is a continuing renewal of energy and will and ideas.

This is all to say that education must not only be about the technology of our journey. It is important, very important, that we can travel in shuttles rather than Model T's. It is very important that we can feed the masses by farming only one percent of the land. It is important that we can keep people alive for the journey with new cures as we engage in a biomedical race with the ever-adjusting microbes. But what shall we make of this splendid journey? What is it possible for us and our culture to become? The moral imperative of education is to teach people to take seriously their freedom, and like Clemenceau said, to recognize that freedom "is nothing in the world but the opportunity for self-discipline."

In times of turmoil, there will always be plenty to condemn. We live in an era of the politics of siege. By election time, every two and four years, the landscape has been left desolate by the dust storms of rhetoric which leave our eyes burning, our belief in our leaders shaken, and our confidence in our nation somewhat disillusioned. We get caught up in the politics of destruction. The health of any democracy will not be tested by whether we bring our anger and disappointment to the polls but whether we bring our minds and our resolve and our hope. As a nation or as individuals, we will not be sustained by negatives. An education must be about helping us figure out what we are for, to take the risks of shaping new agenda and conceiving new possibilities in our communities. It is imagination that will make industries flourish and cause civilizations to be reborn. The moral imperative is for people to understand that each of us bears a genuine measure of responsibility for what the world becomes.

The genius of a university should not be simply to educate abstractly. We ought to help people sense the larger measure for their lives—to think more seriously about their prospects for hope and whether it is possible to find some measure of resilient joy. We have learned long ago that no amount of education will make us feel good. The genius of this institution should center about bringing thought and freedom together. The moral imperative of education springs from our capacity to take what we have learned, to take hold of the power of thought along with the capacity to be free and to bring them both to bear upon human decisions.

So, the moral life does not spring from following someone's code of behavior—whether that code was delivered by Hammurabi or Moses, Jesus or Buddha. Blind followers are not the hope of democracy. These codes turn out to be lessons of what thought and freedom are likely to compel us to do. But achieving moral perspective is quite another matter. Cultivating a moral perspective does not have to do with joining any person's religion or belonging to anybody's church. Morality springs from taking seriously our own claim to freedom and our own commitment to pursue the truth. We should be bold enough to say to students that it is not enough to know the truth. The good life springs from doing the truth, taking what you know and bringing it to bear on what you decide to do.

How on earth can we do that at Mercer or Yale? We achieve that end by coming to terms with our larger calling. We are not here to educate the multitudes. We can educate a few folk who can enter the world of work, the world of politics, the world of family as people who combine competence with a wider understanding and a wider embrace of their responsibility for improving the human condition. The educated person will be less quick to put down other people's ideas and more prone to act with respect toward other people's cultures. We must educate people who have thought about the challenges to the sanity and civility in our world and in our workplace. The truth is that we are on the journey of civilization but we are not civilized yet. If you wonder about that, look at the Middle East or our own political processes where we become buried in the dust storm of negative and destructive rhetoric.

Our challenge, indeed our genius as a university, must be to give to our students not only the most rigorous, the most disciplined of educational expectations, but to help them achieve a measure of self-transcendence. We should do it by combining technique with critique, by combining calculus with philosophy, by combining textbooks with Great Books, by requiring students to struggle with actual problems that are tearing at the fibers of our society. Strange as it may sound, we should craft educational programs that are peculiar to our character as a university. We have the capacity to combine competence with compassion, reason with prudence, an understanding of what the world is like with a vision of what human life together could become.

Therein lies our genius. The genius of the university is to educate people who can think, think carefully, think caringly, and think critically. We should educate people who take hold of the power of thought and who treasure their capacity to be free persons. And, finally, we need to educate people who are sufficiently self-transcendent that they can grasp the power and influence of their own presence and their own imagination in the world. Enlightenment, compassion, and imagination will bring light to communities whose dreams are stalled or whose politics have grown stale.

I am convinced that our problem is not that we think too much of ourselves, but that we think too little of ourselves. We do not fully comprehend the power of our presence here. Our goal among the constellation of students and faculty is to set them free to make a difference and to sense, moreover, that making an important difference in the world of work, in the world of finance, in the world of politics is a moral imperative of being an educated person.

- 8 -

Peddlers of Hope

A university is a congregation of folk who, in very different and distinct ways, become peddlers of hope. They are people who care, who light lanterns to help us see our way, who set out beacons by which a culture can discern the difference between ways that lead to progress and those that lead to decay. The yearning to educate lies deep within the human spirit. We are all seeking enough light to live more wisely, more humanely, more healthfully. We want to make better choices, more principled judgments, and to relate to one another with more integrity and respect. A university education helps people not to become trapped by the way things have been.

Each fall the eagerness and energy combined with the uncertainty and anxiety of beginning a new year of college is a sight to behold. There is nothing quite like the opening day of school. School years are bracketed with celebrations—convocation on one end and graduation on the other. If you ever wonder about the worth of the enterprise we call higher education, slip into the back of one of these gatherings. In those places, you get a full sense of the expectation and achievement that provide energy, momentum, and life to a university.

When I say that a university is a constellation of peddlers of hope, I mean to underscore three things about the work of a university.

1. First, *education represents the regenerative capacity of our culture*. Societies decay. Organizations decline. Ideas wither. Without an education that probes the boundaries and chips away at unsolved problems, our culture begins to grind

to a halt. We cannot live forever on yesterday's achievements. Either we keep learning and discovering or we begin to drift into a spiral of decay. Civilization can never be placed on autopilot. We can too easily slip into behavior that is uncivil and inhumane. The vitality of any society must be regenerated over and over again. Education generally and higher education specifically is the most powerful force in our culture for renewal and progress. The values of a society cannot be preserved simply by embracing them. They have to be recreated. If they are to hold, they will have to be embraced not only because our parents embraced them, but because we have decided that they are true and right for our time. We cannot sustain ourselves on our forebearers' commitments alone. We must generate our own commitments. Education is the arena where we claim the genius of our heritage and create our future.

2. Secondly, *education harnesses the power of the imagination*. Education provides a context for a conversation between experience and imagination. Experience may indeed be life's best teacher, but experience alone is not enough. Learning means combining experience with untested ideas and unwarranted hypotheses. We know, of course, that imagination that is unharnessed can become nothing more than fanciful daydreaming. Add discipline to imagination and we have the beginning of education. Disciplined imagination is thought's most powerful ally, an ally that lays the foundation for both logic and poetry.

Children are born with the wonder of imagination. The journey of learning is not about laying aside the imagination in favor of more "true and tested" answers. The journey of learning is about cultivating the capacity to discipline our imagination so that every individual can bring their unique gift to the world in which they live.

Education is the arena in which experience and imagination can talk as friends.

3. Thirdly, *education is about making connections*. We live by connecting, connecting with our history, connecting with problems to be solved, and relating to one another. Every new discovery is about uncovering new and unseen connections.

The university is an environment where hope is born by connecting with new ideas, by pushing back the frontiers of knowledge, by probing new approaches to understanding human problems, and by becoming more tolerant of people with different histories and different values.

The university is a laboratory for learning that an individual and a society is the fabric of connections. All real living is relating. Tear us away from our relationships with family and friends, with ideas and commitments, and there is nothing left.

Education, inevitably, transforms how people connect. It changes how they meet one another, how they understand or relate to themselves and how they engage the world.

Socrates said it this way: "The unexamined life is not worth living." The work of the University is the examination of living, and by living, I mean connecting. If we have not connected with people and ideas, we have not known the joy of learning or the hope of living.

Throughout the diversity of our remarkable institutions of higher learning, we find students and faculty, teachers and scholars for whom learning is changing who they are, what they do, the goals they will pursue, the values they will embrace. Hope rarely resides in the emergence of a superhero who will come on the scene to solve all the problems we face in our world. Hope more likely resides in whether you and I and the people we teach can find the intelligent will and the moral courage to act in heroic ways.

The goal of teaching and learning in a university is to enable the people who study and learn and teach here to become bearers of hope—people who have the intelligence and the courage to make our world a better place.

9

The Starry Heavens Above and the Moral Law Within

Immanuel Kant, a prominent eighteenth-century philosopher, wrote of his own preoccupation with "the starry heavens above me and the moral law within me." Kant was one of the turning minds of Western thought, a figure comparable to Sir Isaac Newton. The passion of Kant's mind symbolizes the course that higher education should pursue. For those of us engaged in the daily chores of teaching and learning, it is important to recall the global dimensions of our work. The issues to which Kant addressed himself remain the questions of mankind—understanding the universe in which we reside and probing the mysteries of the moral and inner life. I speak of neither science nor morality in a narrow sense. I speak of science rather as the rational apprehension of our world and morality as the principled interpretation of human experience.

A few thousand years of intelligent life leaves us bewildered by both the flood of information that is cast upon us and the boundless mystery that is ever abiding. The pursuit of learning comes by bringing the mystery to bear upon the information. Information alone will not provide knowledge, for information and knowledge are quite different matters. Their reckless confusion causes many misdirections in the course of our work. The mass production of information has created an identity crises for education. That crisis stems from our treating the aims of education as the dissemination of information. Information and knowledge are importantly related, but they are also importantly different.

This confusion seems to be further complicated by the enormous social change that is being experienced in our society, indeed throughout the world. Our nation has moved from a nation of farmers to a nation of laborers to a nation of clerks. The industrial revolution largely replaced our fundamentally agrarian society. The strategic resource for a farming society was land. The industrial revolution changed all of that. In an industrial society, the strategic resource is not land, but capital. We seem to be living in the throes of moving beyond an economy dominated by industry and manufacturing to one that is dominated by information. The workers of an agrarian society are farmers. The workers of an industrial society are laborers. The workers in an information society are clerks. The farmworker was measured by his energy and endurance, the laborer by his skill, the clerk is sorted by his access and facility with information—the manager or administrator being only a more sophisticated version. For the first time in our history, there are more clerks than laborers in the job force. Manufacturing is in decline as the stalwart of the American economy. The sun is rising on information industry. Most of the workers today make their living processing information, with computers and microprocessors being their most important tools.

Education faces these fundamental changes with some uncertainty. The focus of education is on the pursuit of knowledge. But we are unclear about the distinction between knowledge and information. The primary and secondary schools are also unclear. With the industrial orientation, the counterpart to knowledge was vocational training. With the emerging information orientation, educational institutions are quite naturally becoming preoccupied with information and how to process it. But schools should not be viewed primarily as information dispensaries. That task can be performed more efficiently through television and home computers. Education is in the knowledge business. We are about helping people learn how to learn, to connect information.

It is not enough to drench our students with data. They must learn how to interpret, relate, and transcend the data. They must judge the data. Knowledge has to do with learning, reason, inquiry, experimentation, hypothesis, observation, testing, deduction, and presupposition. Information pertains to data, its collection, storage, and retrieval, and combinations of the same.

Education has always dealt with information, hence the confusion that information is its soul. In fact, in earlier decades, information was often restricted to the educated. But today, information is more abundant, which only means that the use and abuse of information makes the task and responsibility of education more grave.

Our access to information is outstripping our ability to understand. Understanding is a child of learning and knowledge. Educators cannot afford to become mere transmitters in the information network. The task of educators is to "make sense" of the network, to restore the discipline that is required to integrate the oversupply of information into a whole understanding of the world and our place within it. Our aim then is not solely information. It is understanding. Information serves us as a tool.

As we are attracted toward the siren sounds of information, we must be sure that it does not become the sacred shrine of education. Information must be used in the service of knowledge. For, in whatever age, agrarian, industrial, or information, knowledge and learning remains the center of human progress. Knowledge requires the rigors of logical rationality, the eloquence of dispassionate inquiry. It is in the

coming age of information accessibility that we must underscore most clearly the need for learning.

The pursuit of knowledge provides its own intrinsic
worth. The values of education are found not only in what is
learned but in the process of learning itself. The application
of reason to experience means that we do not become managed and manipulated by the sensory data that breaks upon us.
Learning and knowledge enables us to judge and to assess our
experience, to gain some distance between what happens to us
and what we cause to happen. The work of the university is to
protect and enhance the distance between information and
judgment. The distinction is critical to the proper function of
the university and identifies our most serious contribution to
the people we serve.

In the course of the universe, we are yet infants along the
way. My judgment is that the learning place should not still
the probing eternal questions that spring from birth. Our
greatest gift may be the uncertainty of it all, the splendor of
our world of worlds, laced with the tragedy and the pain.

We who teach serve those who ask. For they remain our
best hope. The hope of the human order will not be best
served by the mere assimilation of more data, but by the
disciplined inquiry that enables us to achieve at least a
tentative understanding of the world about us—of the "starry
heavens above and the moral law within."

10

In Praise of Ideas

The university finds its soul and its substance in the life of ideas. Insomuch as the discourse of ideas becomes replaced by the mere forms of education, the university withers and loses the essential power of its existence.

Most of us entered the arena of education because we were captured ourselves by the beauty and significance of important ideas. We saw a human mind able to reach beyond the mundane to the essential. We began to see the world not as a collection of frenetic activities, but as a systematic and meaningful whole. We became students of the life of reflection.

The university stands in every human community as a celebration of this life of reflection. It is a sanctuary from the daily traffic of making a living and negotiating relationships to the more transcendent act of thinking and probing the reasons of nature itself. In this sense, the university is not a place to remain. The university influences the larger human order chiefly through its students who find within its boundaries a place to stand aside and to consider critically their own presence and place in the world.

Education occurs on at least two levels. We come to the university in order to learn the skills that will enable us to cope with the world more effectively. Put more bluntly, we learn to exploit the world more skillfully. We study to become workers, to become parts of the social fabric that blend and fit into the corporate needs. The university in its diverse schools is a place to become more highly skilled and more technically proficient in a wide range of human endeavors. But the university must also help its students to transcend the very technical and professional skills they are seeking to master.

We need not underestimate the value of knowledge itself, even technical knowledge. You cannot transcend what you do not know. The university aims toward both knowledge and understanding. We need more, not less, proficiency. And we must add to that knowledge a place and a time for understanding the larger connections that constitute our world. Somehow we must see together that the world is not a collection of discrete people and objects dangling together in a void of time and space. Every person bears a connection with every other and the manner and spirit in which we live together is of fundamental importance.

Transcendence should not be viewed as withdrawal. The point of transcendence is to be able to see our interdependence and relatedness more clearly. The exploitation of our proficiencies without reference to fundamental connections among us makes us into mere drones, uncivilized, without meaning or significance. The goal of the university is to help us integrate our learned skills and competencies with an understanding of our own presence in the world.

It is possible, of course, for a university to abandon its commitment to ideas. When that happens, it becomes only another training ground devoid of reflective insight. The issue then is not whether it shall become a good university, but simply whether it shall become a university at all.

This commitment of ideas must, of course, be reconstituted in every era. Even though we have repeatedly celebrated the university's history, we also bear responsibility for shaping what the university becomes. Amidst the mundane activities that consume us even as educators, we need to keep our vision high and our prospects noble. Excellence will not reside in numbers. It is not even whether we shall be the richest. The achievement of excellence rests more within than without. It rests within whether we will expect of ourselves, of those who study here, of those who teach, and of those who administer, a high devotion to principle and integrity.

The pathways toward excellence are not esoteric, hidden away in some deep catacombs. Excellence requires first that we be a university where ideas flourish and where people matter. And, it requires that we be a place where freedom of thought, intellectual honesty, and the presentation of beliefs are conditioned by a respect and tolerance.

In my judgment, the continuing measure of the quality of any good university will be its ability to cause its students to grapple with the great ideas of human history. The university is not a place to deliver to our students a bundle of ideas already tested and sealed for their acceptance. The university is not an antiseptic environment, sterile and safe from the dangers of dispute. The university is a place where concepts are in conflict and where new ideas are born. It is a place where the mind is enriched and the capacity for reflection is strengthened.

If we are to be worthy of the call to excellence, we must hold high the commitment to ideas as a torch in the night. I do not refer to ideas here as mere abstractions. I use ideas as the most general substance of which an education is formed. It is ideas that free us from the limitations of specific, discrete events. Except through the efficiency of ideas, we could look at the heavens but we could never explore them.

In our educational endeavors, we are concerned for at least three kinds of ideas. I refer to these ideas as *aesthetic* ideas, *analytic* ideas, and *constructive* ideas.

By "aesthetic" I mean the ideas of perception. The educational process refines and broadens the perceptions of human experience. There is an understanding of the world that comes simply by becoming more aware of the context in which we live. Education should enhance our understanding of immediate experience. It should help us understand what we are already seeing and hearing. The educated person, then, sees the world more thoroughly, more fully, even more intensely. Our task in a place of learning is to help one another see the world with understanding. It is insight for which we aim, seeing not only disparate elements but interrelated parts.

The act of learning helps us understand that the world does not exist as an empty datum, merely to be observed as a foreign object. We are very much engaged with our world, and our relationships turn out to change the very substance of reality. Our exploration of space and our explorations of the atom are rooted in the ideas of perception. We are driven to know the essences of things, not merely to encounter the world, but to understand it, to gain our bearings as voyagers on Planet Earth. The role of a university is to teach us not only look but to see, not only to listen but to hear. We may call it appreciation, understanding, or comprehension. By whatever name, the process of learning strengthens and refines the human sensibility. We receive the world more fully into our experience. It is a matter of perceiving beauty, even when it is marred by ugliness, of sensing wholeness even in the presence of brokenness. The very essence of the university lies in awakening our aesthetic sensibilities.

Education is also concerned with what I choose to call here "analytical" ideas. Rigorous thinking uncovers the implications of the ideas we hold. Some people would wish to diminish the value of analytical knowledge as being purely redundant.

Knowledge by analysis is not so much concerned to know more about the world by perception as to peel back the implications of what we already understand. For teachers and students, the university is a context for critically examining the logical implications of the ideas we hold. If we are to be a good university, we must hold high the power and place of reason. We must be willing to follow the paths of logic, unafraid of logic's revelations, and unthreatened by reason's limitations.

The highest achievements of human civilization have been uncovered by the exacting exercise of thought. We educate in the confidence that the tragic human conflicts that devour us must be placed under the analysis of reason. We cannot assume that reason will cure every human ill. It clearly will not. But we cannot be content to bob adrift in a sea of propaganda, propaganda either under the guise of political rhetoric or pious prophecy.

The work of the university is to make critical thinkers of us all, to make us less subject to the vagaries of half-baked and frivolous talk. When we look at the developing nations on this little isolated planet spinning steadily around the sun, we become frightfully aware of our deep dependence on the power of reason and the enormous importance of reasoned restraint among the people of Earth. The conflicts of human-kind are rooted in the strong commitments to very different ideas and we must find ways to reason together if we are to be able to survive together.

The university is also a place for what I call here "constructive" ideas. Constructive ideas reflect the confluence of perception and creativity and analysis. Civilization will be affected by those who study here today. The progress of humankind may be quite literally dependent upon our ability to frame new thoughts and to construct fresh ideological alternatives in every profession, and in every discipline. In every aspect of the social order from economics to politics, we must be searching for new ideas to guide our work and our behavior. The world has not become so well ordered that we need only to preserve our successes. Human civilization is still in its infancy and there is no guarantee that the human race as we know it is here to stay. We may end up killing one another in the name of peace. More than ever before, our world requires competent thinking about alternative directions for human society and a will that is good enough to endure the conflicts that exist among us.

Therefore the university must be concerned not only to understand and to analyze, but to create new alternatives and to form new ideas for charting the prospects of our life together.

The achievement of excellence requires that we make "ideas"—aesthetic, analytical, and constructive—the center and focus of our work. And beyond the exploration of ideas, it will require that people matter. That people matter should not be translated as sentimental rhetoric. The university is not a place that pats heads and offers bland assurances that everything is going to be okay. To the contrary, the university is a place that takes human life seriously and offers a retreat for deciding what values will dominate our living. The university is a place to come to grips with the meaning of human life, not only personally, but as the people of Earth. The ruptures of human community that occur in our world affect us all individually and personally and those eruptions of killing and bitter battle can never finally be solved by mere reactionary hostility. We live on this small complex globe together; and whether we like it or not, we live together as a family of men and women.

Caring for people begins here in our own context in a university. We must learn to be concerned not only with what a person knows, but what a person becomes; to be concerned not only with the human mind, but the human will. People are our greatest resources for solving the problems that plague us, but these same people, angry and uneasy, are the greatest threat to human survival. If Earth becomes only a silent and barren rock in the universe, it will not likely be because of a massive Mount St. Helen or a descending glacier, but because we have devastated one another. It is only fear that is likely to drive us to that destiny. The university can be a place to replace fear with understanding and to find new ways of interpreting our desperate need and interdependence upon each other.

Being a good university will also require the intellectual honesty that reflects itself in patience and tolerance. Being a university that affirms the integration of faith with learning places a special burden upon us. We are first of all responsible to insure that our commitment to reason is not compromised by the religious heritage of the university. We are equally responsible to insure that the religious heritage of the university is not diminished by intellectual arrogance. The search for truth should never be compromised by the presentation of belief and the affirmation of belief need never disvalue the search for truth.

Intellectual honesty requires us to acknowledge that the human order of things is shaped not only by what people know, but by what they believe. Excellence will never require the expulsion of belief. It will require the tolerance of dissent and the respect for diverse human commitments. The university is a setting where any ideas, religious or nonreligious, may be probed with impunity. It is a place where we may admit our doubts and inquire into our uncertainties. It is a place where people come together not because they think the right thoughts or hold the right creeds, but because they are bound by a mutual commitment to human inquiry, human dignity, and human respect.

Excellence will often elude our description, but we will know it when we see it. Though we may not have the courage to confess it, we also know when we have been content with shabbiness in educational performance. William James once said, "College education should help you know a good man when you see him." As a good university we will know excellence when we see it, and we can afford to aim for nothing less. Its achievement will never be an easy task. It cannot be done by administrative decision or by faculty committee. Its achievement must be reached by the university as a corporate community.

The future of our country, indeed our world, does not rest in its machinery or in its technology. I am convinced that it lies in our intelligence and in our moral strength. We can best measure our steps by the disciplined reason that we expect, by the principled judgment that we inspire, and by the hope of goodness to which we cling.

11

Undergraduate Education Matters

You and I are born connected, and all of us, from birth, become a part of a journey toward becoming more fully human, toward finding the meaning of our particular presence in the world, and even toward hearing what I will refer to as "a calling" that echoes deep within the recesses of each person's life.

Our human journey destines each of us to be a learner. Apart from active and engaged learning, we are mostly like empty clay shells, passively being molded, but unable to speak with a sense of personal authority that springs from within. In our earliest years, our learning is largely unstructured—sounds and sights that find their way into the space we occupy. As we grow, our learning becomes more structured. We begin to be educated more formally.

Our lower education sometimes can seem to become a grand scheme of manipulation. Our structures for learning become increasingly rigid, with tables to be memorized and curricula to be mastered. But, in general, we educate for the common good. We set out a common curriculum of history and science, and mathematics and literature to serve as the foundation for tutoring young minds.

I have no quarrel, indeed, with the rigorous pursuit of established curricula except perhaps that they should be more rigorous and less distracted by the paraphernalia of the social context. That is, we at times appear compelled to muddle education with a curricula that includes such things as instruction in driver's education and sex education and how to interview for a job. We become preoccupied with offering courses on alcohol abuse and drug abuse and the effective uses of birth control. All of these subjects warrant some attention, no doubt, but I think it is a mistake to presume that everything a youngster needs to know should be taught in the public schools. I say the schools ought to forget teaching driver's ed and sex education and how to be a parent. Let the Department of Motor Vehicles or the church or the Wednesday Club or would you even believe the parents teach them how to drive or be a parent or how to make love more effectively. Schools do not really make good surrogate parents.

Education, I believe, is first and foremost about helping to enable every person to become a person, to probe and to exploit their resource bank of talent, and to reconnect, in imaginative and compelling ways, with the world from which they sprang.

This journey of connecting, in my judgment, does not begin by looking outward. I believe the journey of relating is first and foremost an inward journey. Fostering, inspiring, cajoling, and facilitating, and encouraging that journey may be among our highest callings as educators, particularly as educators in an undergraduate context.

The whole struggle of growing through adolescence becomes mostly consumed with understanding ourselves over against parents and friends, finding our place over against established traditions and taboos. Self-preservation usually comes as the first order of business of parents, teaching our young the rules of the road. We teach them the socially acceptable ways to act, to dress, to speak, to wear their hair and to stand in public. We teach them how to belong and how to fit into the social fabric.

And then we send them off to the university for higher education where they may be met more with higher training than higher learning. There our disciplines have multiplied and we are faced with gifted professors who literally know more about their subjects than anyone on earth and their goal often is to recreate their students in their own image.

Here students also enter the world of the core undergraduate experience. In my view, the goal of this common educational experience should be to rescue the journey of learning from an enterprise that produces well-educated students who have never been set free to hear the interior voices that will ultimately tutor them toward a sense of purpose and hope. I believe it is not enough to produce competent engineers or superb accountants or effective counselors at the bar. The result of such a goal, standing alone, would be to produce practitioners and professionals who are well trained but who have never visited the intersection of who they are and what they do. I regard this intersection of who we are and what we do to be a holy place where one ought to put a stone and build a temple. And if we have not been to that intersection in our lives, we are likely to suffer from a kind of empty careerism that leads inevitably to the traumas of burnout and self-doubt.

The truth is that many, if not most, of our programs of general education are neither general nor educational. They are a set of politically negotiated courses that insure every discipline's turn to "show and tell" in the competition to recruit majors. The field of general education has, in large measure, sacrificed the common learning space to the academic political landscape where elaborate academic duels take place in order to demonstrate academic might. Politics prevail over teaching and learning.

During the Kennedy administration, Arthur Schlesinger left Harvard to accept an appointment in Washington, D.C. When asked why he would leave his prestigious post at

Harvard, he replied, "I have decided to leave Harvard and go to Washington in order to get out of politics for a while."

The president of Columbia was heard to report that academic politics is the most vicious of all politics for two reasons:

- The stakes are so small.
- The people of honor are always outnumbered by the people of principle.

Harland Cleveland who served as dean of the Hubert Humphrey Institute at the University of Minnesota was, back in the turmoil of the Vietnam era, the newly elected president of the University of Hawaii. When asked why he would go to lead that institution where the turmoil was at its highest—marching and daily protests, often on the verge of violence—he said, "If you are going to have trouble, you might as well have it in good weather."

Well, the weather is frequently stormy for you people who are sharing the cause of a common educational core. And the predictions are not for the weather to get much better. Politics will continue to prevail in powerful ways, sometimes even erupting into violent storms. You and I must work to enable the essential mission of the educational experience not to become lost, amidst the cacophony of disciplinary priorities that consume our universities and their resources.

In all candor, I believe that the most persistent source of our problems may be an undereducated professoriate and the ignorance of people in charge. Esoteric scholarship is better compensated than the scholarship of leading students to probe enduring and thorny issues, even though these issues turn out to shape the human spirit and affect dramatically the well-being of human culture.

Again, the value and contributions of scholarship should certainly not be diminished. But neither should it be seen as the defining and ultimate issue of the academic enterprise. I actually believe that we would probably do well to require our first- and second-year faculty to participate in a core learning program. It is very difficult to expect that the teacher who has never made that long and disarming journey inward to find the courage to mentor another in such a journey.

The preoccupation with our "discipline-centric" professional careers can become a means of avoiding the inner and more difficult questions that bubble up on the human terrain. We define our careers and finally ourselves by the discipline we serve. Take away our disciplines and we have no way to center our lives. The discipline becomes the defining essence of our being here. Take the discipline away and all is emptiness, "Vanity of vanities, all is vanity."

I suspect none of us need look beyond the boundaries of our institution to find clear and tragic examples of colleagues who yearn to recover or to find for the first time a purposefulness about their work. They long for a purpose that they actually bring to their work instead of relying upon the work itself as the sole provider of meaning and purpose. Freedom is hardly something they actually experience—intellectual freedom, yes, but the freedom to be, the freedom to reconnect with the inner life has been lost to the shadows, lost in the abyss of "discipline-centric" definitions of what it means to be a teacher.

Teaching without connecting is akin to the breaking of day without the rising of the sun. It is surprising how often the notion of intellectual freedom is used to refer to the right to probe the outer world without encumbrance, yet the same freedom is not claimed to probe the depths of inner experience.

While we might use one of any number of works, let me refer to Martin Buber as a way of framing my point. Actually, I believe that Martin Buber has much to teach us about teaching. The lesson of *I and Thou* is not the lesson of duality. The lesson of *I and Thou* is the lesson of the ultimate power of relatedness. The "I" of the teacher is realized only in meeting the "Thou" of the student. The mantra of teaching should be Buber's affirmation that "all real living is meeting" and where there is no meeting, there may be abstract instruction, we may even find the rigorous but mechanistic training of the mind, but we will find nothing so elegant and engaging as teaching going on. Above all else, teaching is a relational event. And a relational event worthy of the moniker "teaching" is not an agent/patient encounter.

The world we call teaching is a radically different calling. The calling of a teacher is born of the intimate, powerful, and transforming experience of connecting. In Buber's metaphor, the "I" of the teacher cannot be born without the "Thou" of the student.

The recovery of the power of relating, in my view, belongs to the mission of a general-education program. A core text such as *I-Thou* becomes a vehicle for navigating the organic cellular structure of teaching and for negotiating the powerful inward journey of learning.

The I-Thou is not the connecting of an "I" and a "Thou." No, the relation is primary. The action is in the hyphen. There is no "I" without the "Thou" and the "Thou" only becomes an "I" in the mutuality of the relational event. If an instructor wishes to become a teacher, she must look within to find the Thou that makes it possible to hear the calling to teach.

I use this reference to suggest that we are all children of relatedness. Our life-form itself is an issue of relatedness. When we observe another person, what we really observe is what I have chosen to call a "region of behavior." Something we call a person is actually an extrapolation, an exemplification of certain relationships. It is not the case that we exist and then we relate. Our presence is an expression of our relatedness. Apart from relating, we do not exist. We are nothing. We are not a person in relation, or a person who relates. We do not create relationships. Relationships create us. A person is a window for seeing and understanding the constellation of relationships that shape the substance of what it means to be a solitary individual. The solitary individual is an abstraction and to regard a solitary "I" as an essential entity is what Alfred North Whitehead would have called "misplaced concreteness."

While the individual—that is, the individual as student or the individual as teacher—should not be seen as the primary unit of reality but more as an extrapolation of reality, the way into this constellation of relationships is more inward than outward. That is to say, we understand the "Thou" component of our being here not by dissecting and analyzing the other over against which we stand, but by having the courage to take the most strenuous and difficult journey into ourselves.

Every journey inward takes us into our essential relatedness. And it is in the inner zone that we are able to catch a glimpse of the connections that create our particular presence. The intersection of those connections also constitutes the substance of what I refer to as our own unique calling. In other words, the only truly unique aspect of our being here, the only individuality we possess is our unduplicated and singular "calling."

I use "calling" here in the broadest possible sense. It is a poetic term to refer to a particular and profound intersection of connections that occurs only once in the world. DNA, for example, is an exemplification of that intersection of connections but not an exclusive one. Our relatedness or our peculiar constellation of connections is the only "nonclonable" aspect of our being here. That aspect of our being here called DNA is only one component of our relatedness, albeit a major and defining component of the set of connections that constitute our identity.

In probing the discussions of our relatedness, we can consider several macro levels of human connectedness. Those macro levels include

1. our connections within, our inner relatedness or how we relate to ourselves;
2. how we relate to other people; and
3. exploring our connections with the world.

As individual persons, we are not isolated or independent from the vast universe that embraces us. You and I exist among the stars and this enormous expanding universe of about fifteen billion years belongs to the fabric of our interior lives. Any sense that we possess a standing independent of the galaxies is simply mistaken. We are profoundly and inextricably bound up with this universe of light and darkness to which we belong. We belong to its matter and energy and that belonging also teaches us something about our presence here.

We are not discrete organisms in the midst of a lifeless, inanimate world. We contribute to the energy of the universe and in all of its vastness, no other fragment of the constellation of energy and matter bears the precise capacities that we bear. In the universe we embody a cauldron of talent unduplicated in all of the vastness that lies before us. We are not objects located in an alien world; we are subjects defined by the world's embrace.

The most intimidating connections of our personal lives is the overlap of our lives with the lives of other people. In our personal experience, two boundary conditions bear upon us most intimately. Those two boundaries are death and the inescapable presence of another person. The mystery of death is a boundary which we approach with considerable symbolism and ritual. You and I live between the "not yet" and the "no longer." And those boundaries of the "not yet" and "no longer" turn out to be powerful connections that influence and shape the in-between.

Just as awesome a boundary is the boundary condition of another person. In this case, we are connected, we interact, we are dependent upon, we partner with, we are subject to, we meet with respect or with prejudice the unfathomable presence of another person. Sheer fear causes human beings to try to connect with others through control, manipulation, and other forms of power. It is our human effort to control, to name the mystery. Yet, despite all of our efforts to manage the existence of the other, we cannot gain control over their inner being. We can manage them, manipulate them, even kill them, but we cannot eradicate the singularity and the limitation they impose upon our being here.

The forces of control are actually ways of denying or trying to eclipse our interconnectedness. The relatedness of persons is the ontological predecessor to the existence of the self and the other. We are nothing without the human embrace. Fear deafens our capacity to hear the calling of the other that lies within us. Setting ourselves over against the other becomes ultimately a self-destructive act. The enduring truth is that we belong to one another and one of the most serious challenges of learning is to be able to open ourselves to the power of relating with openness and integrity. It is a process filled with risk and vulnerability, but it is the only process by which an individual can claim the meaning of being free.

Finally, the way into the essential connectedness of our lives does not lie among the vastness of the heavens or trying to find our way through the unbreachable "otherness" of the Other. Author and Teacher Parker Palmer points us in another direction when he tells us that "Vocation does not come from a voice 'out there' calling me to become something I am not. It comes from a voice 'in here' calling me to be the person I was born to be, to fulfill the original selfhood given me at birth by God." The place to meet the "Thou" of the universe and the "Thou" of the other person is within.

The searching of our core undergraduate experience is not, after all, ultimately about the texts we study. It is about what the texts expose and illuminate about the human spirit. The texts probe difficult and enduring dilemmas and confront human conflict. Yet, in the final analysis, the text is about bringing us light and hope—the almost desperate longing for hope that lies only half hidden behind the shroud of confidence, even arrogance of those we teach. Our work is about enabling people, faculty, and students alike to once again become learners, to enable them and us to see and to hear the gifts with which we arrive in the world and which we spend the early years either abandoning or letting others replace with their own controlling definitions which they would like to impose upon our lives.

Allow me one more citation from Parker Palmer:

In families, schools, workplaces, and religious communities, we are trained away from true self toward images of acceptability; under social pressures like racism and sexism our original shape is deformed beyond recognition; and we ourselves, driven by fear, too often betray true self to gain the approval of others.[*]

I commend to you that the high purpose, or, if you will, the "calling" of our teaching is to ensure that higher education does not simply provide higher training as the follow-on to lower training. There is indeed an important place for higher training in the undergraduate experience. Yet our calling lies elsewhere. It is nothing less than assuring that the human spirit is set free, that every person is set free to hear his or her calling, and that every person is set free to understand the inner truth that is illuminated by the light within.

Our work as educators is to be lanterns of light, helping persons define the meaning of their being present in the world. Your calling and mine, our high and noble calling, is nothing less than to help young men and women find their way toward becoming more fully human and to become better citizens of the world, to become free, and in their freedom become light and hope for a new generation.

---

[*]Parker Palmer, *Let Your Life Speak: Listening to the Voice of Vocation* (San Francisco: Jossey-Bass / New York: John Wiley & Sons, 2000) as excerpted in *YES! Magazine* (Spring 2001).

12

Civic Engagement

The University is committed to becoming a leader in the arena of civic engagement. Our focus on civic engagement arises from the pull of social responsibility and the push of recognizing the physical and historical setting of the University. Since 1871, Mercer has been developing its campus and programs on what was the western edge of the City of Macon and the end of College Street. No doubt when the leadership of Wesleyan College was exploring a move to a more suburban environment, the comparable leadership within Mercer University surely explored a similar strategy. Every institution is obligated to examine its own circumstances and priorities, and the responsibility of each board and administration is to determine the best course for the development of each institution. Through some combination of inertia and wisdom, the proportion of which has been lost to history, the University administration and board of Mercer University chose to remain on College Street and Coleman Avenue where the formerly western edge of the City was rapidly being drawn nearer to the heart of the city center. Working and middle-class neighborhoods were bustling and downtown was still the center of commerce.

After the Great War, demographics had begun to change. The rush to the suburbs intensified in the 1950s and 1960s. Downtowns began to decline as large malls sprang up, and hamlet shopping centers began to emerge all across cities. In Macon, public housing, in those years segregated by race, was developed within blocks of the University, and the traditional middle-class housing stock began to decline as more of it was purchased by absentee owners. The area around the University became more economically depressed, and the downtown corridor was faced with having to redefine its future as storefronts were abandoned, and the economic viability of downtown began to erode.

The response of the University to the changing demographics and the economic decline of the area surrounding the University was chiefly to turn inward, becoming more of an enclave for teaching and learning, a proverbial ivory tower. As a result, the University became more isolated from the community, sometimes resorting to building fences with barbed wire, in order to insulate itself from a declining neighborhood where property values were eroding and crime was increasing. Conversely, the neighborhood grew increasingly suspicious of this large institution, which literally towered over the neighborhood, and tensions between the neighborhood and the University grew. Detente, more than engagement, was the order of the day.

A few years ago, the University with considerable care and deliberation, began to conceive and to implement a radically different strategy for relating both to the neighborhoods and to downtown. This strategy may broadly be described as "civic engagement." One of the real challenges of the new strategy is to implement such an approach while holding on to the important reality that the University is also a learning place that transcends the community. While being a good neighbor, the University must remain a sanctuary of learning, a place the currency of which is ideas and debate, where social norms are both respected and challenged, where respect for diversity of thought and intellectual freedom is continually fostered. So, the idea of civic engagement is not to toss aside our calling to be a community of scholars and teachers and learners, but to pursue inquiry and useful knowledge while taking a measure of responsibility for our neighborhood and becoming a unique resource for community development.

Several steps have been critical to the development and implementation of this new strategy of civic engagement. Early on, the University hosted a prayer breakfast in the President's Dining Room to which we invited neighborhood leaders and residents. We discussed the goal of joining hands to solve common problems, quite uncertain about where these conversations might lead. We made clear that the University was not promising to have all the answers and certainly had no intent to be in control of the neighborhood. We were, rather, extending a hand of cooperation and partnership, offering to be a catalyst for community redevelopment.

In order to undergird the University's initiative and to secure the University's commitment to be a better neighbor, in 1998 we formed the Mercer Center for Community Development, now the Mercer Center for Service Learning and Community Development (MCSCD). The Center applied for a federal grant to assist University/Community partnerships. In the second year of application, the University received one of only a few such grants awarded in the nation, particularly to private universities. Since that time, the Center, working with the University Advancement office, has subsequently been the recipient of additional grants from foundations, the federal government, and private corporations, such as the Federal Home Loan Bank of Atlanta, to facilitate community redevelopment, including a major grant from the John S. and James L. Knight Foundation. MCSCD has continued to coordinate the effort and has become the major interpreter within and outside the University for Mercer's implementation of a strategy for civic engagement.

One important initiative that has paid significant dividends has been a program to assist faculty and staff who purchase houses in the neighborhood. Working with the Historic Macon Foundation, the University began providing a stipend for any faculty or staff who purchased a house in Huguenin Heights. The program has been very successful, and we have watched neighborhoods on the northern edge of the campus that were deteriorating in property values and were plagued with increasing crime rates become transformed into a strong and viable neighborhood with increasing property values, dramatically reduced crime, and about fifteen faculty and staff who have become homeowners in neighborhoods immediately adjacent to the University. The initiative was then broadened to include Tattnall Place, a neighborhood across from Tattnall Square. The University has now adopted this policy for houses being purchased or constructed on the other side of the campus in an area known as Beall's Hill, a gateway neighborhood to downtown. The signs of the transformation of that neighborhood are now becoming visible. The University participated with the Macon Housing Authority and the City of Macon in applying for and receiving an eighteen-million dollar U.S. Department of Housing and Urban Development grant for the demolition of public housing known as Oglethorpe Homes to be replaced by townhouses two blocks from the University. These developments are only some illustrations of the leadership and contribution of Mercer's MCSCD.

We should underscore that the value of civic engagement is far greater than the obvious practical benefits, which are mutual for the University and for the community. Perhaps the most important benefit lies in what civic engagement means for the academic community of Mercer University: community partnerships advance learning and create more civically engaged graduates.

Above all else, the University is a deep reservoir of intellectual capital. We often underestimate the value of the people resources of the University. This institution hosts a substantial and remarkable constellation of talent. The University is rich in intellect, imagination, creativity, and energy, and this cadre of talent can be an extraordinary resource for community redevelopment. So, one of the contributions which the University can make is to apply the richness and breadth of faculty and student intellectual capital in helping to solve real and pressing community problems. In the process, the community receives the benefits of a well-spring of thought and imagination that has incalculable value in addressing difficult problems. At the same time, the faculty and students are able to put their own ideas and energy in the service of solving real-world human problems.

This expanded initiative has already seen valuable "action research" from faculty, who applied classic marketing analysis to the marketing of affordable housing for home ownership in Beall's Hill, to a senior design team in Industrial Engineering, who designed a system of evaluation for management of maintenance in the housing authority facilities. For a number of years, Mercer freshmen in the First-Year Seminar Program in the College of Liberal Arts have tutored second- and third-grade students at John W. Burke Elementary School in the neighborhood. Burke School, with almost all its students on free or reduced lunch, was recognized two years ago as a "No Excuses" School of Excellence for its consistent performance in the top twenty-five percent of schools in Bibb County. Our faculty and students can make a difference, not only across the state and nation, but right here in our backyard.

In addition, Mercer's commitment to civic engagement helps to foster a new range of skills and attitude among its students, its graduates, and indeed the entire University community. Students and faculty and staff are encouraged to conduct their lives and their work in a manner that take seriously the call of civic responsibility. In the final analysis, our nation can be no stronger than the values of its citizens and their willingness to make a difference in the character of our communities. Democracy, more than any other form of government, requires the leadership of informed and responsible citizens. I am convinced that we will have fully met our obligation as educators only if we create citizens who are able to see themselves as responsible stakeholders in the lives of their communities. Therefore, I believe that civic and political participation is a good to be fostered among those who study and learn at Mercer University.

Students can learn about very specific mechanisms that are likely to be effective in tackling difficult community issues, ranging from public health to education to economic development. Civic engagement enables them to learn that effective community leadership requires the ability to listen with more care, to speak with more understanding, to respect people who come to conversation with different perspectives. We need to help students develop the skills to negotiate differences beyond impasses that often cause community initiatives to be stalled or ineffective.

John Dewey reminded us that democracy and education are inexorably intertwined. Indeed, the idea of democracy is founded on the assumption that free people will make rational decisions. It follows that education is a critical resource to the survival of the democratic spirit. Civic engagement brings together in the academy the threads of thought and action in weaving a fabric of academic reflection and civic responsibility. It creates a partnership between service and learning.

When Mercer's students graduate, we know one thing for sure, life will not come to them in the neat disciplinary packages that we experience in our University studies. Life is not neatly demarcated into Biology, and History, and English. Life and work are always interdisciplinary. The exercise of civic responsibility and the strategy of civic engagement place a premium on the value and the usefulness of collaboration. The solution to the most persistent human problems that beset us always requires a community of thought and action. Civic engagement enables us, both as a community of learning and as individuals, to link together the power of disciplined thought with the power of a creative imagination. We believe that civic engagement broadens the reach of the classroom and enables the world and the communities in which we live to become places of learning. Our challenge, as educators, is not only to help students learn to think independently, but to help them learn to collaborate as partners in addressing the most serious civic and moral concerns of our time.

So, at Mercer University, we have added to our "curriculum" a commitment to civic engagement. And by so doing, we are improving the economic and cultural health of our community, and we are preparing our students to become more effective stewards of their own social responsibility.

13

Thought and Compassion

I see myself as an educator, a philosopher, a theologian. My work as an educator flows from my life as a philosopher and a theologian. If that all sounds rather Olympian, I do not mean it so. In more personal terms, I mean to say that I am a minister, a teacher, and a person absorbed by the wonder of it all. I have been asked on many occasions if I do not grow weary and frustrated by the criticism and controversy that is a part of the work of a university chief executive. Obviously I have no magic exemption from fatigue. But I do not tire of who I am or what I do.

Each of us has a special journey on which there are abundant joys and some burdens. But the wonder of the journey has not, for me, been eclipsed by the periodic sting of conflict. We are larger than the events that impinge upon our lives either as persons or as institutions. We should never permit some event, whether felt as pain or gladness, to become the single lens through which we see ourselves or the world—even the way we view God. The wonder of being here—the wonder of knowing and relating—should never be reduced to a narrow or myopic understanding of our human situation.

It is sometimes hard to keep the larger perspective. Yet it is only the larger perspective that can save us from fatigue's despair. We belong to a holy order and to a history that is not easily thwarted. As naïve as it may sound, I believe that, in the end, good will prevail. We have only a faint vision of what that good is or what it entails. But we do carry a portion, even a small portion, of responsibility for seeking the course of wisdom and fostering good among humankind. We must look for worthy ends for our lives and for our institutions. I

believe that our highest and most noble calling is the cultiva-
tion of the twin gifts of thought and compassion.

As persons who bear a responsibility for educating young
people, we carry a special responsibility for the importance of
thinking. Taking thought in a disciplined and critical way is
indeed one of the high and worthy ends of our educational
endeavors. Thinking is rooted in our yearning to know, the
curiosity that awakens even as an infant rambles through the
closets and pantries. Curiosity lies near the base of learning—
the compelling impulse to open up the insides of the world
around us. The proclivity to discover is like unwrapping all
the packages of mysteries that are strewn about our human
pathways. The more we open, the more that seems to lie
before us. Aristotle was right. He told us centuries ago that
"all persons by nature desire to know."

How do people learn to think and how do they effectively
enter the search for knowledge? They do so by reading and
listening. They do so by pondering and reflecting alone about
what they are reading and observing. The discipline of
reflective solitude should not be underestimated for its
contribution to learning. The capacity for critical thinking
often relies heavily upon the willingness to cultivate the
discipline of reflection. Unless we are willing to draw aside,
to ponder what we have studied, we become students only of
the conversations and the texts. That is to say, the words of
learning become our focus instead of the subjects and the
realities which the words and the lessons convey.

Learning is a deeply personal affair. The aim of learning
is to engage ourselves with the ideas and the issues that have
shaped and are shaping our world as well as to engage in that
more personal struggle with what we think and believe. In the
process of learning, objectivity and subjectivity become
intertwined.

Reflecting, however, is not sufficient to the process of learning. Learning to think also requires a sense of mutuality. "Community" perhaps is the right word but it is almost a word that has been taken from us because of the inclination to regard it as a group of persons who hold common ideas and who act with a common will. A university is not a community in that sense.

A university is a community of learners where openness and the capacity to listen as well as speak marks the learning environment. We learn to think with each other. Thinking with each other both encourages us and keeps us honest. Our ideas, our affirmations, and our doubts do not exist in a vacuum. We are defined by our relationships and neither our ideas nor our uncertainties exist outside the context of being related to each other. Thinking requires interaction. If we are not prepared to engage others in debate or in mutual affirmation, we are not prepared for critical thinking.

The university is a place for encouraging and facilitating the development and the wonder of thought. It is the place where we live and in which you and I are deeply invested. We treasure the importance of thinking and the power of thought in making people whole and in fulfilling the highest prospects of human civilization. It is a high calling.

In my judgment, education is not only about thinking. It is also about caring. That is probably the greatest contribution to be made by a good university that was founded by a group of people who called themselves Baptist. They taught us that life is not only about knowing; it is also about loving. St. Gregory was near the heart of the matter when he wrote, "Love itself is knowledge; the more one loves the more one knows." On the other hand, the philosopher of science Michael Polanyi speaks of the personal commitment that belongs to and is a part of the "hardest" of the "hard" sciences. He writes:

> I have shown that into every act of knowing there enters a passionate contribution of the person knowing what is being known, and that this coefficient is no mere imperfection but a vital component of his or her knowledge.*

A part of the power of truth lies in the passion that prompts our pursuit and the creative impact of our discoveries. Compassion is both the prompting impulse and the creative outcome of thinking. Without the power of compassion in human experience, the power of learning lies lifeless and sterile on the landscape of our lives. It is a way of saying that we do not work at achieving an understanding of truth as objective and dispassionate knowers.

Dispassion in the search for truth is instrumental. The end of knowledge is the passion to care and to serve our common good. Knowledge enables us to celebrate our connectedness with the world around us. The notion of compassion or love in this context refers specifically and precisely to this connectedness. That is to say, love is not used here in any sort of sentimental or even emotional sense. It is used to convey the relatedness that is so essential to our world. Knowledge alone makes an object of the world to which we belong. Knowledge controls and often makes the world serve our ends and purposes. When we see the world another way, taking seriously the reality of love or relatedness within the world,

---

*Polanyi, *Personal Knowledge: Towards a Postcritical Philosophy* (Chicago: University of Chicago Press, 1958; corr. ed., 1962).

the purpose of knowledge is transformed into a force which enables a person or a society to fulfill its higher prospects.

One goal of education is to keep thinking and loving linked together. Knowledge disconnected from caring easily falls prey to abuse. The power of thought which maintains a commitment to the responsibilities for loving enables us to stay in touch with our connections with one another and our world—connections which give meaning and purpose to the world.

One final image for describing my point. In the nineteenth century, the German philosopher Ludwig Feuerbach said that we are what we eat.[*] In other words, we are what we consume.

Feuerbach may have been wrong. What we consume only determines in part who we are. It is no small part and that part should not be discounted. But the whole point of our kind of educational endeavor is to say that we are not only what we learn; we are what we teach. We are not only what we take; we are what we give. We are not only what we consume; we are what we invest in. Relatedness is the heart of the matter. Good education, I believe, should strengthen our ability to think and enrich our capacity for love.

---

[*]"Der Mensch ist,was er isst," that is, "Man is what he eats" (1850).

14

Lessons on Leadership

Leadership is not a spectator sport. In your business or your organization, in our community or our University, at times we are all called to be both leaders and followers. A leader is simply an individual who takes initiative to solve a problem. The truth is that leaders are not established by rank or position, power or wealth. The mantle of leadership is no respecter of rank or position. Either we take initiative to solve problems or we do not lead.

I have watched leaders up close for a generation. And I want to report here what I have learned from observing leaders in action. (Yogi Berra said, "You can observe a lot by watching.")

I have learned that there are certain distinct traits that mark every leader. So, I have noted five characteristics that are present in every leader whose work I have observed and then relate to you some of the lessons about leadership I have learned along the way.

Trait 1. Developing Relationships

Leadership is first and foremost about relating. There are no isolated, unconnected leaders. Leaders are people who embrace the habit of connecting. Relationship building is often ceremonial. If you want to lead any organization effectively, it is wise to remember the power of symbol. Most of our relationships are nurtured by ceremony. In my case, it has to do with recognizing the power of ceremonial events such as graduations and convocations. But every endeavor, every business, every organization, every church, every family is held together by the power of ceremony. It may be coffee.

It may be an employee recognition dinner. It may be a note that says thank you for work well done.

Most of our human interaction is mediated by symbol— the power of language, a letter, a word of encouragement. The rhythm of our relationships belongs to the heartbeat of leading.

Trait 2. Solving Problems

Managing, administering, and solving knotty problems that plague your business or our university always lies near the center of leading. Solving problems is the down-in-the-trenches, hard work of struggling with the substance of what we do. Leadership is never simply about cheerleading. Leading is about the disciplined, focused, and rigorous work of facing into the winds of frustration and anxiety. It means sorting through the challenges we face and defining solutions that work in real time and in the real world. Problem solving is the deep and hard work of leading.

Trait 3. Developing Resources

Leaders are resource developers—financial resources, human resources, idea resources. Resources form the boundaries of every institution, of every business. You will never be better than your people, and your ability to develop your resources, to increase your revenue, to inspire your people will be a critical component of any successful leader.

In my arena, resource development also means fundraising. I tell people that I raise money for a living. And I love raising money. I never mind asking people to invest themselves and their resources in Mercer University. I had rather ask for a million dollars than a thousand dollars. It takes no more time and it's a lot more productive.

But, of course, I believe that giving enriches the people who give. On one occasion, I was visiting in Jacksonville,

Florida and I was meeting with a gentleman asking him to consider a gift of two million dollars to the University. He agreed and after our meeting we were having lunch. During lunch I began to talk about philanthropy and indicated that I had observed that people who were, by disposition, able to give were usually healthier and happier people than those who could not give. Some folk are so possessed by their possessions that they cannot let go. They are clutching, possessed by their wealth.

A few weeks later, I was in the office and I had a call from my friend and he said, "Kirby, would you tell me again how good I am supposed to feel." I said, "Jack, if you don't feel good, you haven't given enough. I do not want you to give until it hurts; I want you to give until it feels good." Leading is about developing resources.

Trait 4. Thinking

The most neglected task of leadership is the power of thought and imagination. You cannot lead effectively unless you are willing to preserve time to think about what you are doing and where you are going. Leaders must continually reimagine what is possible. Great leaders are those who set others free in their organizations to be mavericks, to think the unthinkable, to challenge the undoable, to conceive new solutions to old problems. Einstein was right when he said, "Imagination is more important than knowledge." We all become victims of the way things have been. Leaders set us free to reimagine the world. So, whatever you do, don't forget the power of thought.

Trait 5. The Courage Factor

Every leader must have a measure of the courage factor. There is no way to solve problems—political, social, economic—without engaging the courage factor. Leaders turn out to be people who will act even when they cannot see their way with absolute clarity. Courage means being willing to take risks, to consider new ideas, break down old barriers and push back outdated boundaries. The road of leadership is not paved with certainty. Leadership always takes us through the valley of risk and uncertainty. There are sharp turns and steep hills. There will be bruises and bumps. But leaders do not define their lives by the bumps and bruises. Leaders define their lives by the problems they solve and the integrity they embody. Solving problems and living with integrity always requires courage.

So, remember the traits of leadership. They will be replicated in every successful leader.

1. Developing relationships
2. Solving problems
3. Building resources
4. Fostering thought and imagination.
5. Embracing the Courage factor

Now, let me tell you a few lessons I have learned along the way.

Lesson 1. Every person is the business. I have learned that every person makes a difference because how somebody views your organization is determined by the work of that one individual. Back when switchboards were more commonplace, I told our switchboard operator who was retiring that she was the most important person there because she influenced the perceptions of thousands of people whose idea of Mercer was shaped by her voice and her spirit. If there is a job that doesn't matter in your business, you need to get rid of it. Every person is the business, taking responsibility, making tiny, sometimes trivial decisions, taking ownership. Every person matters. Every person counts.

Lesson 2. Be careful what you die for. Don't be crucified on a six-inch cross. Some people are like Eric Hoffer's "true believers," always ready to die for every cause, ready to join every parade, to carry every banner. My observation is that our problem is not that people have too few principles. They have too many. My admonition is: Have fewer principles and take those more seriously. Most steps forward are made though systematic and prudent compromise. Know what it is for which you will go to the wire and negotiate all the rest. Most steps forward are made though systematic and prudent compromise. Be careful what you die for.

Lesson 3. You and I live and work between what I call the "not yet" and the "no longer." There was a time when you were not yet in your place of work or leadership. And there will be a time where you are no longer in that place. You and I live and work in a window, bounded by the not yet and the no longer. In that window, that frame of influence, what matters is what value did I add. What problems did we solve? What difference did I make? You cannot live in someone else's time and space. It is not our job to solve the problems of the next generation. Your responsibility, my responsibility, is more focused and closer to home. The issue is, between the not yet and the no longer, what difference did I make?

Lesson 4. I am learning that leadership is not about making yourself more powerful. Leadership is about making the people around you more powerful. Leadership is too often viewed as garnering power and influence. It is a mistake inspired by hubris. The real art of leadership is helping other people release the creative power of their own presence in the business. All around you are the people who can make you look good, the people who can make you rich. Empower them. Lift them up. Set them free. The best leaders provide the least control and the best direction. Leadership is not about gathering power; it is about giving power, giving other people the capacity to use the power of their being here.

Lesson 5. Talent and ideas will prevail. When I look for associates in the University, I look for bright, hyperactive, articulate, overachievers. Talent will prevail. It sometimes seems that getting ahead depends upon having the right political connections. While internal politics may from time to time enable a person to ascend a few rungs on the ladder of success, don't count on it. As a strategy for getting ahead, it will fail. Trust competence. Put your money on talent. Rank and position may determine who speaks, but talent and ideas will determine who listens. Talent and ideas will prevail.

Lesson 6. I have learned that a decision doesn't have to be perfect to be good. Leadership is far more about making good decisions than perfect decisions. Neither time nor understanding generally allows us to make flawless decisions. Making good decisions is about gathering the best information available and reaching within yourself for the best will you can muster, make a decision and let it go.

Balancing your head and your heart is very important. Learn with your head; listen with your heart! Use your head and your heart but don't let your heart cause you to lose your head. I am reminded of the gentleman who outlived two wives, one named Millie and the other Tillie. When he died, his family asked him, did he want to be buried next to Millie or next to Tillie? He replied, "Bury me between Millie and Tillie, but tilt me toward Tillie." When you make a decision, listen to your head and your heart but tilt your decision toward your head.

Lesson 7. Listening and learning are the keys to leading. No person knows enough to stop learning and when leaders stop learning, they begin to lose their ability to provide competent or wise leadership.

On one occasion, I was asked the most important lesson I had learned as president of Mercer. I replied that I had learned that more problems are solved by listening than by talking. Listening is about taking people seriously and treating them with respect. Very often, a conversation between two people is no more than two monologues. Two people talking, nobody listening. Instead of listening we find ourselves thinking about what we are going to say when they stop talking. Conversations occur with lots of people talking and few people listening.

Leading is about listening. It is the only way to convey authentically and persuasively that every person matters. In our business or in our community, learning and listening will be the keys to leading.

Finally, let me add that if you want to lead any endeavor—your business, your church, your community, your family, you have to "pace" yourself. I use PACE as an acronym to remind us of four truths.

P = Priorities. Know your priorities. You cannot climb every mountain. You cannot conquer every disease. You cannot heal every hurt. You cannot solve every problem. It is better to solve some problems than to dream of solving every problem. Know your priorities. Write them down and let them direct your course.

A = Autonomy. Know yourself. Develop a sense of autonomy. Decide what is important to you. What are the core principles of your life? What is your center? Without centering yourself, knowing yourself, knowing your strengths and your weaknesses, you will be adrift—tossed about by the last person that got to you. People will stand in line to tell you what to believe, where to live, how to vote, and what to do. Amidst the competing calls for your devotion, find a center, a sense of being a person, a sense of autonomy. It is as old as

Socrates. He said, "Know thyself." Leadership requires autonomy.

C = Collaboration. Achievements are rarely accomplished alone. Link up. Connect. Leadership is not about having the right connections. It is about making the right connections. Collaborating, connecting, is about pooling human resources. Teams are always more powerful than individuals. Collaborate. You will get more done. Share the limelight. Good leaders see the light. Great leaders spread the light.

E = Energy. Leadership requires stamina, discipline. Leadership is hard work. It means working when you are weary, working on a problem even when others have given up. There is no magic. Leadership requires stamina, the willingness to work through the night, to walk through the shadows of uncertainty.

I have watched it for a generation of college students. The difference between overachievers and underachievers is rarely talent alone. Talent is critical but talent alone is not enough. The overachievers are those who combine talent with discipline. Leadership requires discipline, energy, stamina, hard work.

So, if you want to lead, remember to "pace" yourself.

Know your priorities.

Know yourself, know your center.

Learn to collaborate.

Be prepared to work harder than everybody else.

- 15 -

Creating Our Future

As we stand on the threshold of a new century, we are facing new questions about what is to become of us—our society and our civilization, our businesses, and our universities.

It is, of course, the business of the future to be uncertain. Abe Lincoln was reported to have said, "The best thing about the future is it only comes one day at a time."

In all our businesses, I believe we must either take responsibility for our future, for shaping the alternatives that lie before us, or become victims of old behaviors. The future is not something that happens to us; the future is something we create. Whatever has made us successful in the past, will not alone make us successful in the future. Today's heresies will be tomorrow's truths.

So, I want to offer here some clues to the future that are emerging in the world around us; you and I are entering a new era in which knowledge is exploding and the world markets are inextricably tied together.

The first clue: Everyone is connected.

We face today a dramatic rise in the power of technology. Distance is dead. The power of technology, through the internet, pagers, cell phones, PDAs, e-mail, and faxes, are a part of our everyday life and yet, only a few years ago, no one had ever heard of e-mail or faxes. These new technologies are changing the world in which we live. The power to navigate the world at the click of a mouse is changing every corner of our lives. Products with intelligence built into them are emerging all around us. Smart phones, smart cars, computers that remember your preferences. The power of that technology will only increase in the years ahead. Humans will have more mechanical and electronic parts; machines will be able to think more like humans. The margin between person and machine will begin to get murky. Everyone is connected.

We used to be connected more slowly. Highways, letters, even airplanes. People would write letters and think better about mailing them. Today, people write e-mails and push the "send" button and often feel a gnawing anxiety that it should not have been sent.

In 1943, Tom Watson, chairman of IBM, said there is probably a world market for about five computers. In 1977, Ken Olson, president of Digital Equipment Corporation, said he could foresee no need for anyone to ever have a computer in their home. In 1996, there were 200 million computers in the world, and in the year 2000 there were 500 million computers in the world. Today, it is approaching a billion.

Net-education and cyber-students will transform the learning landscape. In 1996, sixty-five percent of all workers were knowledge workers. Now, more than ninety-five percent of all workers are knowledge workers. Digital illiteracy will cripple a person's ability to advance in the years and decades ahead.

You and I live in a debris of data. Data is the unorganized sludge of the information age. We are covered up with data. The challenge that lies before us is to translate all the data that is rushing toward us into useful information. Even more importantly, we must transform information into knowledge, that is, information that can be used to solve problems. Knowledge is information put to productive use. Information alone can be the enemy of intelligence.

*The second clue: The twenty-first century
will be the century of the woman.*

In the first place, there are more women than men. Not because more women are born than men, but because the survival rate for girl babies is much better than it is for boy babies. Women are a stronger breed, and they live longer than men. In the world of education, we have discovered that they are brighter and that women are better learners than men. In fact, boys are four times more likely to drop out of school than women.

When we say that women are brighter than men, let me be a little more specific. What we are really saying is that the bell curve is tighter for women than for men. That means that there are more men in the world who are geniuses, but that there are a lot more men in the world who are stupid.

In 1970, there were 400,000 businesses owned by women. *Fortune Magazine* recently ran a cover story on the fifty most powerful women in American business. More than ten million businesses are now owned by women. Women today account for more than 3.3 trillion dollars in consumer and commercial spending every year. Three out of four healthcare decisions are made by women. Two out of three healthcare dollars are directed by women. Sixty-five percent of the car-buying decisions are made by women. (Today only seven percent of the auto salespersons are women, but that will change.)

In 1970, one percent of the business travelers were women; in the year 2000, fifty percent of business travel was done by women. By the year 2050, fifty percent of the chief executive officers of major corporations in this country will be women. Why is that true? In order to be competitive, companies, corporations, and organizations have to recruit the best talent that is available for them. If they systematically exclude half of the talent pool, mainly the talent pool of women, they simply will not be able to remain competitive.

The third clue: Global really means global.

There are no longer any isolated economies. We are facing radical changes in the marketplace. In 1996, the U.S. trade was 1.8 trillion dollars; 836 billion dollars in exports and 950 billion dollars in imports. Ultimately, if we are to flourish, that imbalance must be corrected. One billion dollars in exports equals 14,000 jobs in this country.

By the year 2020, the largest economies are likely to include: number 1, China; number 2, the United States; number 3, Japan; number 4, Indonesia; and number 5, India. There is only one in this hemisphere, namely, the United States. For the first time in human history, anything can be made anywhere and sold everywhere. The workplace will change. Workers who have Third-World skills will be paid Third-World wages, even if they live in the First World. A bridge to a more global economy is being developed through regional trading blocks. Jumping from national economies to a one-world economy is a leap too big to make at once, and so there are emerging trading blocks such as NAFTA and the European community. There are no isolated economies. Global really does means global. Old boundaries are crumbling and they will never be reconstructed.

The fourth clue: The most serious threat to face
human civilization is not the changing global market.
It is the rise of terrorism.

Terrorism that is both domestic and international is more exportable and more powerful than it has ever been. A few vials of a biological toxin could kill the entire population of a small city in only a few weeks.

This threat to civilization is genuine and real. No longer is terrorism a fact of life for other remote nations of the world. Terrorism is domestic as well. There are terrorist activities throughout the world, including Ireland and Bosnia, Israel, Jordan, Iran, Palestine, Saudi Arabia, Afghanistan, Kenya, Oklahoma, Birmingham, Atlanta, New York, Waco.

Let me mention two reasons. One is the rise of religious fundamentalism throughout the world. Fundamentalism is a social volcano erupting in every major religion in the world— Hindu, Muslim, Jewish, Christian. Across the world, those persons who have lost out economically or politically, who cannot make the system work for them, retreat into religious fundamentalism, where a world of certainty replaces a world of uncertainty. They preach that if one follows their rigorously prescribed route, they will be saved; otherwise, they will be lost in the sea of uncertainty. It is an avenue of hope. People can live longer without food than they can without hope.

The perpetrators of the bombings in Atlanta a few years ago called themselves the "Army of God." Terrorism. A Presbyterian minister who killed an abortion doctor said that he knows he did the right thing. He was obligated by God to kill. In all cases, there is very little difference among Christian, Jewish, and Muslim fundamentalism. It is nurtured by the same spirit and seeks to reverse moral decline by imposing a religiously prescribed social order. This problem is not short term. Most of the terrorism of religious fundamentalism lies ahead of us, not behind us.

The second cause of terrorism is poverty. The population is booming in the world's poorest countries. The gap between the rich and the poor is growing greater every day. There are approximately 180 member nations in the United Nations; 160 of those nations are radically poor, where about 20 of those nations are rich. Poverty breeds fear, fear breeds anger, and anger breeds terrorism. Unless, as a civilization, we learn to lift others up from their poverty, we could become defeated by our own wealth.

The fifth clue: People are living longer and healthier.

By the end of the next century—with increased exercise, gene therapy, biotechnology, replacement parts—it will not be uncommon for the average life span to be 120 years. By the end of the new century, there will be genetic tests for risks of cancer, diabetes, strokes, and heart disease, along with prescriptions of gene therapy. Medicine will be tailored for your individual genetic makeup. We are facing major changes in the way people live. The metaphor of the twentieth century was the atom; the metaphor of the twenty-first century will be the gene.

I have five rules that will add fifteen years to your life and mine. They are simple. They can be done by everyone in the room:

(1) Do not smoke.

(2) Wear seat belts.

(3) Exercise regularly.

(4) Seventy percent of what you eat should be fruits or vegetables.

(5) Live with grace. Bitterness, resentment, and trying to get even will shorten your life.

The sixth clue: As we approach the next century,
we are facing major shifts in the age and color
of the world's population.

Our populations are becoming more diverse. By the year 2030, the world population will increase from 6 billion to 8.5 billion. That's an increase of 2.5 billion people, and 2 billion of that 2.5 billion will be born in countries where the daily earnings are less than $2.00.

Our U.S. population is becoming more Native American, more Asian, more Hispanic, and more African American, in that order. Hispanics today make up nearly thirty million people—eleven percent of the U.S. population. Today, they have overtaken African-Americans as the nation's largest minority population. By 2020, half of America's youth will be "minority." We are importing the poor.

In addition, our populations are getting much older. The fastest growing age group in the United States is 85 and older. By 2050, the number of persons 100 years or older will be almost a million. The population of developing rich countries is getting older. The population of underdeveloped poor countries is getting younger. Today, those persons in the U.S. over 65 account for thirteen percent of the population. By the year 2030, they will account for almost twenty-five percent of the population, soaring between now and then from 33 million to 69.5 million. Where today there are 4.5 workers available to work to pay for every pension, in 2030 there will be no more than 1.7 workers available to be taxed to pay for every pension.

Excluding interest on the national debt, half of the federal budget goes to the elderly. The government spends nine times as much per person on the elderly, those who do vote, as it does on the young, those who do not vote. Even so, the truth is this: Nothing is more important to the old than the economic success of the young. We are facing major shifts in population and those shifts will change everything about how our political system and our economic system works.

The seventh clue: Quality is everywhere.

It is the threshold for success. Quality products, quality services, quality education. Without quality we are not even in the game. We have to become obsessed with doing things right. Quality means adding distinctive value.

At Mercer, we must be a distinctive university, with a mission that is clear, precise, and distinctive. In the commercial world, that is called the power of design. The power of branding. Without quality and distinctive value in the next century, we will not compete. One thing is sure about E-commerce, it puts the customer radically in control.

Finally, the eighth clue:
Intellectual property will be the key to wealth
and achievement in the twenty-first century.

By the year 2010, if a person does not have a college degree, he or she will be automatically poor. Education, above all else, is about the capacity to create intellectual property. It is about future leadership and our future wealth.

The fuel of the future will be ideas. I cannot overestimate the power of ideas. Knowledge is growing at an exponential rate. By the year 2020, knowledge, the volume of knowledge in the world, will double every seventy-three days.

Education cannot just be about new configurations of information. We can get information on the Internet. It has to be about thinking new thoughts, creating new solutions to old problems. It is about learning to be persistent learners. Earning power will be inextricably linked to learning power. Knowledge will become the new basis for wealth. This has never been true. In the past, wealth was based chiefly on ownership of natural resources, plants, equipment. "Owning" knowledge is very different.

So, let me conclude with three suggestions about facing this new generation, where we are being catapulted forward toward enormous changes.

First, we must recover the power of the individual person. We have to learn that, above all else, it makes a difference that you and I are here. No one hears what you hear or sees what you see, stands where you stand, can think what you can think, can do what you can do. No one lives where you live. Our calling, yours and mine, is to live out our particular gifts in the world, because no one can replace any of us. We do not need a society of clones. Every person is the organization. We need every person's individuality, we need every person's personality, we need every person's mind and talent, every person's creativity, every person's imagination, every person's passion, every person's discipline.

Second, corporations, institutions, schools, and communities must break through the boundaries that have become barriers, the ways things have been done. We must begin to reimagine ourselves. Every corporation, every community, every school needs a futurist group, a group that celebrates the mavericks, fosters the courage to try new ideas, to become pioneers in old organizations.

Third, politics will not be the key to the future. Politics is important, but not determinative. Politics is having a terrible time keeping up with the will and the momentum of society. Government cannot show us the way. We must show the way to governments.

But, I am also thinking about the politics of organizations. You have seen it, where people try to move up in organizations through political manipulation and maneuvering. That will be an unpredictable and unproductive method of trying to achieve in the years ahead. Sure, there will be a few people who succeed by manipulation, but I believe that the future belongs to talent—people who bring together the combination of imagination and discipline.

I have watched college students for a generation. The difference between overachievers and underachievers is rarely talent alone. It is more often discipline, the ability to focus on a goal.

The business of the future is to be uncertain. It is our responsibility to create a future that is guided more by intelligence than ignorance. That will require four things:

(1) Imagination, vision. (Einstein said that "Imagination is more important than knowledge.")

(2) Competence, talent. (World-class education will be necessary if we are to be knowledgeable leaders.)

(3) Discipline. (The willingness to focus.)

(4) Stamina, energy. (The willingness to work hard.)

We can create our future, a future where people flourish and where people and cultures connect more creatively. If we have the will and the energy, we can create a future of hope and promise. The mantle of responsibility falls squarely on all of us.

The decades ahead will bear witness to our determination and will to think more creatively, to care more deeply, and to work more persistently to bring order and understanding, freedom and justice, compassion and hope to this small living space we call Earth.

Above all else, creating a future of hope will require courage. The Courage Factor will be the engine of our progress.